D0837858

SALVATION

INCARNATION
Jon L. Berquist

PEACE
Walter Brueggemann

SALVATION
Joel B. Green

SABBATH AND JUBILEE
Richard H. Lowery

COVENANT
Steven L. McKenzie

PRIESTHOOD IN ANCIENT ISRAEL
William R. Millar

Kathleen Philipps

SALVATION

JOEL B. GREEN

CHALICE
PRESS
ST. LOUIS, MISSOURI

© Copyright 2003 by Joel B. Green

All rights reserved. For permission to reuse content, please contact Copyright Clearance Center, 222 Rosewood Drive, Danvers, MA 01923, (978) 750-8400, www.copyright.com.

Bible quotations, unless otherwise noted, are from the *New Revised Standard Version Bible,* copyright 1989, Division of Christian Education of the National Council of the Churches of Christ in the United States of America. Used by permission. All rights reserved.

Cover and interior design: Elizabeth Wright

Visit Chalice Press on the World Wide Web at
www.chalicepress.com

10 9 8 7 6 5 4 3 2   06 07 08 09 10 11

Library of Congress Cataloging–in–Publication Data

Green, Joel B., 1956–
    Salvation / Joel B. Green.—1st ed.
        p.   cm. — (Understanding biblical themes)
    Includes bibliographical references.
        ISBN-13: 978-0-827238-31-2
        ISBN-10: 0-827238-31-2 (alk. paper)
        1. Salvation. I. Title. II. Series.
    BT751.3.G73 2003
    234—dc21
                                                            2001000773
                    Printed in the United States of America   CIP

CONTENTS

Introduction
1

1 Being Human, Being Saved
9

2 Yahweh, the Healer
35

3 Yahweh, the Liberator
63

4 How Can We Be Saved?
93

5 The Community of Salvation:
Then, Now, and the Future
119

Scripture Index
147

INTRODUCTION

I want to know one thing, the way to heaven—how to land safe on that happy shore. God himself has condescended to teach the way: for this very end he came from heaven. He hath written it down in a book. O give me that book! At any price give me the Book of God! I have it. Here is knowledge enough for me. Let me be *homo unius libri*. Here then I am, far from the busy ways of men [sic]. I sit down alone: only God is here. In his presence I open, I read his Book; for this end, to find the way to heaven.[1]

With these words, John Wesley, Anglican priest and founder of Methodism, opened his *Sermons on Several Occasions*. To twenty-first-century sensibilities, Wesley's words may be troublesome. We take offense at this apparent reduction of the gift of salvation to life after death, as though heaven were the single, narrow locus of salvation: "Pie in the sky, in the sweet by and by!" We are annoyed by the individualism that seems to reside in Wesley's words, as though Bible reading or otherwise charting the "way to heaven" was something one might do on one's own, as though playing solitaire,

---

[1]John Wesley, Preface to *Sermons on Several Occasions*, §5.

alone with God. Were we to take offense at Wesley on these grounds, though, it would be because we have not located him within the horizons of his larger message and program of church renewal. His understanding of the church was profoundly social, focused as it was on mutual accountability, relational growth in grace, and communal participation and discernment. And he deploys the phrase "the way to heaven" not to restrict salvation to life in the hereafter, but to speak of the life-journey as a whole, a journey marked by growth in grace and faithfulness, a journey whose beginning, middle, and end are mapped in relation to God and God's people.

If Wesley's words seem problematic, this may be because of the caricatures of the message of salvation we have encountered, or which have been inflicted on us. Threats of hellfire and damnation come to mind. Turn or burn! If you were to die tonight, would you be certain that you would go to heaven? Though such exclamations and questions may have been thrust upon us, we should not confuse these with the focus of the biblical theme of salvation. On this topic, Wesley's words are far closer to the mark. We may hear in them two pivotal emphases: (1) Salvation is a "way," a journey, a life-path, and not only or merely a point in time or a destination we seek; and (2) this way of salvation is the focus of the biblical message.

In his little book *Theology: A Very Short Introduction*, David Ford observes that "salvation" is that point in the study of religions in general— and Christian faith in particular—where all the key issues converge.[2] How a community views God, the character of the cosmos and of humanity, the nature of evil and sin, the process of healing and recovery of health, its own life as a community, and its hope—these issues and more come into focus when we address the theme of salvation. If we take seriously that "theme" expresses "a relation of being about," that the "theme" of a text has to do with unifying the many and often distinct and sometimes discontinuous elements of a text,[3] then there is an important sense in which we are justified in speaking of salvation as the theme of scripture. Here is the integrating center of scripture, just as it is the coordinating center of theology.

---

[2]David F. Ford, *Theology: A Very Short Introduction* (Oxford: Oxford Univ. Press, 1999) 101–19.

[3]Gerald Prince, *Narrative as Theme: Studies in French Fiction* (Lincoln: Univ. of Nebraska Press, 1992) 3.

Our understanding of salvation is the concern of that branch of theology known as *soteriology*—from the Greek words *sōtēria* ("salvation") and *logos* ("word" or "an account of"). Soteriology builds on a number of related concepts, including, for example, *anthropology* (our understanding of humanity and the human situation), *theology* (our understanding of God), *christology* (our understanding of the person and work of Christ), *ecclesiology* (our understanding of the church), and *eschatology* (our understanding of the end to which God's work is headed). If our exploration of the theme of salvation is to be faithful to the Bible and meaningful for our lives, it must be sufficient to account for the human cry for healing what is wounded, in personal, communal, and even global terms; and it must provide a vision of salvation that can be reckoned and related genuinely as good news. In fact, what we find in scripture is a virtual choir of voices capable of multiple analyses of human need and the condition of our planet, with each witness sponsoring its own distinct, though not unique, soteriological vision. Our concern will not be to jam each witness into a single box or to silence one voice in favor of another. On account of this multiplicity, the biblical witness to salvation can address itself authentically to communities separated by experience and culture. Likewise, the biblical witness challenges and enables us in our different worlds to reach outside of our lives to transformed images of human health and vocation, and even fosters in our communities the ability to generate language and practices of healing and restoration that reflect and embody the biblical hope of salvation.

In the same way, a biblical soteriology presupposes a *theology*, a certain sort of God-portrait, which is rooted in history, but which precedes history. Those who embrace Christian faith are not free to construct portraits of God willy-nilly, since what it means to be Christian is to locate ourselves in the ongoing story of God's relationship to the whole cosmos, and thus to all humanity, and especially to Israel, as this is narrated in the Old and New Testaments. In other words, our understanding of God's nature and activity is oriented around and shaped by the biblical narratives and the ongoing story of God's work with the people of God. This story of God's project is grounded in the scriptures of Israel, comes to expression above all in Jesus Christ, continues into the present, and moves forward to the consummation of God's purpose and self-revelation in the end. That is, biblical notions of salvation presuppose at the same time that they demonstrate the creative and redemptive God, whose purpose scripture identifies as eternal and ongoing, now progressing toward the ends that God has determined. Consequently, we need a storied approach to our understanding of salvation, one that apportions profound significance to the canonical narrative of God and God's people. To be Christian is to belong to an ancient and ongoing story, whose aims, twists, and turns are shaped in relation to the God of Israel. This is the God who provides an inheritance for God's children, who calls for obedience and honor, and who promises faithfulness and love.

Since Aristotle's classic reflections on such matters, narratives have been categorized as having beginnings, middles, and ends. What of the narrative of salvation? Beginnings are capable of supporting and generating multiple narratives, and so it is with the Bible's beginnings. In the first century, for example, Pharisees and revolutionaries, Essenes and the Jewish elite in Jerusalem, these and other groups within Judaism could each read the story of the scriptures particularly as *its* story. The same could be said of the early Christian movement. The Book of Acts records speech after speech in which Jesus' witnesses work to interpret the gospel of Jesus as nothing less (or more) than the continuation of the story of God's people related in the scriptures of Israel. If we can take 1 Corinthians as exemplary, one of Paul's primary agendas in his work among predominantly Gentile churches was to teach those Gentile Christians to read the story of Israel as their story, or rather to read themselves into the story of Israel. In the same way today, Muslims, Jews, and Christians each look to the beginnings of Israel, in the Genesis account of Abraham, as the beginning of their story. But a particularly Christian reading of the biblical story identifies a narrative begun in creation that passes through Abraham, Sarah, and Exodus, and that necessarily leads to—and in an ultimate way is determined by—the advent of Jesus of Nazareth, whom Christians name as Christ and Lord. In a handful of New Testament texts, Jesus is identified explicitly as "Savior," and still other texts present him in this role even when they do not employ the term. Any exploration of salvation in the Christian scriptures cannot escape the catalog of questions that accompanies this designation of Jesus as Savior, which, together with the Exodus, forms the midpoint, the middle of the soteriological narrative with which we are to concern ourselves.

A focus on Jesus cannot, and is not meant to, bypass the role of the church, the community of God's people, either in salvation itself or in the identity of the church as a community of salvation. Neither is it meant to mask the degree to which the purpose of God in salvation is not self-evident around us, in spite of our claim as Christians, based on good biblical warrant, that the age of salvation is already a present reality. Herein lies the importance of tying our understanding of the church to the message of salvation, of being clear in our grasp of the church's commitments and impulses to mission in the world, and of nurturing a robust hope in the power of God to complete the work of salvation.

Roughly speaking, these concerns provide the outline of this study. Chapter 1, "Being Human, Being Saved," explores selected testimony from the Old and New Testaments to the nature of humanity. Although our history has largely been one of differentiating ourselves from the animal world and locating ourselves in a place of preeminence with respect to the rest of the cosmos, we will see that scripture presents a perspective that is both more modest and less isolationist. "Fearfully and wonderfully made" we may be (Ps. 139:14), and "crowned…with glory and honor" (Ps. 8:5), but the pressing image of humanity in scripture is that of creatures in need of and dependent on God for salvation. Chapters 2 and 3, "Yahweh, the Healer" and "Yahweh, the Liberator," respectively, turn then to the primary character in the biblical story, God, and to God's quintessential role as Savior. With astonishing consistency, scripture presents Yahweh as the one who binds up and heals the wounded (to borrow the language of Job 5:17–18). In Israel's scriptures the almost invariable subject of the verb "to save" is Yahweh. Recounting in Exodus 14 the spectacular victory over the Egyptian army at the Red Sea, the narrator summarizes, "Thus the LORD saved Israel that day from the Egyptians" (v. 30). Likewise, in her song of praise in anticipation of the birth of her son, Jesus, Mary addresses herself to "God, my Savior" (Lk. 1:47). It is therefore crucial to explore not only the Bible's presentation of God as healer and liberator (an identity that, in the New Testament, Yahweh shares with Jesus), but also to examine how the categories of "healing and health" and "liberator" illumine the biblical message of salvation.

Chapter 4 focuses on the question, How can I be saved? At stake here are two intertwined, though distinguishable issues. First, how is salvation mediated? Second, how might persons appropriate for themselves God's gracious work? In the first instance, then, our concern is a large one, moving across the biblical materials, as we examine how God draws near to save. The theology of the temple and sacrifice and the nature of the work of Christ come into particular focus here. In the second part of this chapter, we turn more to the human side of the equation. I say "more" because even our responses to God's saving work are dependent on divine grace and illumination. Put sharply, our interest here falls on changed hearts and changed lives, with the dispositions of our inner characters indissolubly linked to our behaviors in the world, both necessary in the performance of salvation.

Where is this biblical story taking us? What is the "end" of salvation? This is the focus of the fifth and final chapter. Here we work to make sense of the sometimes disparate, sometimes otherworldly and fantastic, images that comprise the biblical witness to "The End." Because this view of the *eschaton* (the Greek word for "end") so prominently casts its shadow back on the whole of the biblical story, and thus on the lives of those for whom the Bible is scripture, our exploration of these issues is manifestly bound up with contemporary life. Thus, our more general concern in Chapter 5 is the nature of Christian progress in and toward salvation and, so, of the character of the community of God's people oriented toward God's historic and anticipated acts of salvation.

All of this talk of "understanding" and theological concepts should not fool us into thinking that the Bible invites us in some superficial sense to an examination of its contents as these relate to salvation. Even if the Bible can be examined in order to see what it says *about* salvation, this does not exhaust the message of scripture on the subject. With regard to salvation, we have to deal not only with grasping theological issues but also with being grasped. Indeed, scripture's own theological agenda has to do, above all, with inducting us into—and guiding us along—the way of salvation. The words of the Bible themselves were generated and shaped in the throes of the formation and transformation of the people of God, and when we embrace those words as scripture we find that we have volunteered ourselves for a life of personal and social transformation.

These ruminations determine and speak to the basic character of this book as an invitation to a journey of salvation oriented toward increased understanding, to be sure, but also to transformed commitments, renewed allegiances, and fresh practices. To address the grand narrative of scripture in a way that takes seriously its essential focus on the journey of salvation is to open ourselves to fresh (and perhaps refreshed) perspectives on the world and, thus, on life in the world. In theological terms, this is sometimes referred to as a "conversion of the imagination,"[4] an illumination that allows us new categories for conceiving the world, for making sense of our experiences, and for directing our lives. As Luke tells the story, this openness is demonstrated by those gathered in Jerusalem on that Day of Pentecost when the Holy Spirit was poured out on Jesus' followers. They inquire, "What should we do?" (Acts 2:37). In the same way, those who gathered around John the Baptist, whether the crowds in general or toll collectors or soldiers, inquire, "What should we do?" (Lk. 3:10–14). Seeing the conventional definitions of their faith reframed in Peter's sermon at Pentecost, or refocused by John's ministry of proclamation and baptism, these persons recognize not only the possibility of fresh answers to age-old questions but also the need for changed behaviors. The question takes expanded form in the words of the Philippian jailer, "What must I do to be saved?" (Acts 16:30). This pivotal question must be spelled out in terms of an awareness of God's enabling purpose and a recognition of God's gracious gift, to be sure, but also with reference to human response and participation.

In other words, in the end God's story must be read as our story. To engage the biblical story of salvation is to hear an invitation from God and to join with Wesley in the quest for heaven. Show me the way! Let us advance on that journey!

---

[4]On the importance of "imagination" in biblical studies and theological discourse, see, for example, David J. Bryant, *Faith and the Play of Imagination: On the Role of Imagination in Religion* (Studies in American Biblical Hermeneutics 5; Macon, Ga.: Mercer Univ. Press, 1989).

1

BEING HUMAN, BEING SAVED

Simply put, "salvation" is the comprehensive term for all of the benefits that are graciously bestowed on humans by God. This definition focuses on two poles: God as the benefactor, and humanity as the beneficiary of God's good gifts.

We should not be surprised by this emphasis on the anthropological focus of salvation, but neither should we exaggerate it. On the one hand, the initial account of creation in Genesis 1 reaches its crest in the creation of humankind. Thus far in this opening chapter of the scriptures, in recounting the work of God on each day of creation, the narrator has employed a consistent literary pattern:

1. Introduction: "And God said…"
2. Command: "Let there/it be…"
3. Report: "And it was so"
4. Evaluation: "And God saw that it was good"
5. Time Marker: "And there was evening, and there was morning…"

Following this sequence of events, the light, sea, sky, vegetation, and eventually "swarms of living creatures" appear on days one to five. Orderly creation comes into being in orderly fashion. That the work of creation reaches the height of its crescendo in the creation of humanity is signaled not only by its being reserved for the sixth day, but also by the narrator's departure from the orderly cadence he has established. The work of this day is not just "good," but "very good" (Gen. 1:31).

Similarly, in Psalm 8, a psalm that extols human dignity in the context of divine glory, the psalmist claims of human beings,

> You have made them a little lower than God,[1]
>   and crowned them with glory and honor.
> You have given them dominion over the works of your
>   hands;
>   you have put all things under their feet,
> all sheep and oxen,
>   and also the beasts of the field,
> the birds of the air, and the fish of the sea,
>   whatever passes along the paths of the seas.
> O LORD, our Sovereign,
>   how majestic is your name in all the earth! (vv. 5–9)

On the one hand, this psalm, which functions within the scriptures as a kind of commentary on Genesis 1, sharply contrasts God's majesty with human insignificance. The psalmist appears baffled that Yahweh's splendor does not completely overshadow the possibility of attending to mere earthlings: "What are human beings that you are mindful of them?" (Ps. 8:4). On the other hand, the psalmist recognizes that the human family finds its true identity only in relation to God. Moreover, in a world that marked differences between royalty and common folk on the basis of family lineage (the accidents of birth, so to speak), Psalm 8 disallows any concern with inherited status. Instead, it attributes nobility to every person. Here again, the prominent place of humankind in relation to the rest of creation is accentuated, at the same time that human beings are positioned clearly in relation to God and the heavenly counsel. Even the nobility of humanity is cause for glorifying God.

---

[1] Some English translations read "a little lower than the angels," on account of how the early versions (Greek, Latin, Aramaic) interpreted the Hebrew *elōhîm* (literally, "God, gods"). Other early versions translated the Hebrew term as "God," however, and this rendering is favored by the context.

Although these texts provide good reason for a soteriology focused on humanity, this emphasis does not tell the whole story. From the standpoint of the biological sciences, the relationship of human beings to other mammals, and indeed to all other animals and the whole cosmos, has become more and more evident in the past two centuries. Such a scientific analysis would not be alien to the biblical creation accounts, for there the human creature is depicted very much at home in the cosmos. Humans are situated in relation to other living creatures in almost every way, so that the fate of the one is tied to the fate of the other. In the New Testament, Paul presumes this relationship in his portrait of the consummation of history, insisting that the restoration of all creation is intimately linked to the salvation of God's people: "For the creation waits with eager longing for the revealing of the children of God; for the creation was subjected to futility, not of its own will but by the will of the one who subjected it, in hope that the creation itself will be set free from its bondage to decay and will obtain the freedom of the glory of the children of God" (Rom. 8:19–21). Not surprisingly, then, the book of Revelation cannot imagine the final deliverance of God's people without at the same time envisioning "a new heaven and a new earth" (Rev. 21:1).

As important as it is that we account for the cosmological scope of God's salvation, it remains nonetheless true that the center of the mural of salvation painted by the biblical writers is occupied by humankind. This is a consequence of what distinguishes the human creature from all other creatures. Evolutionary biology, which might be thought to emphasize more the sameness of *homo sapiens* in relation to other animals, admits the same. From the perspective of the natural sciences, the differentiating marks of the human person would include at least the following: (1) the development of consciousness, (2) individuality within community, (3) self-consciousness, (4) the capacity to make decisions on the basis of self-deliberation, (5) planning and action on the basis of that decision, and (6) taking responsibility for these decisions and actions.[2] Biologist Francisco J. Ayala summarizes such defining elements with reference to the human capacity for ethics— referring not to a particular ethical schema, but rather to "the proclivity to judge human actions as either good or evil"; cognitive scientist

---

[2] This list is drawn from Philip Hefner, *The Human Factor: Evolution, Culture, and Religion*, Theology and the Sciences (Minneapolis: Fortress Press, 1993), 118–19.

Warren S. Brown highlights the human capacity for, and experience of, rich, textured forms of personal relatedness.[3] From the perspective of the Genesis account, human distinctiveness is charted in terms of the creation of humankind in the image of God, human "dominion" in relation to the rest of the world, and the call to obey God. We must return to these considerations momentarily. In later chapters, we will take up again the cosmological scope of salvation.

In both Old and New Testaments, the language of salvation is used in a variety of ways—sometimes to denote bringing help to those in trouble (without necessarily rescuing them from that trouble), sometimes delivering persons from peril, and so on. Throughout, application of the concept of salvation presumes a vision of life in its fullness from which human beings have departed and to which we can be restored. Thus, although late-nineteenth and early-twentieth century optimism gave rise in the United States to a narrative defining the human race, and the world with it, as traversing an inevitable, unrelenting path of progress, this is not a particularly biblical appraisal of things. Although largely discredited by heinous acts of evil most poignantly related to times of war and terrorism in the twentieth and early-twenty-first centuries, this way of putting life together continues to persist, whether in promises of things "new and improved" (read: "newer is better," or "ancient ways are primitive") or in our ongoing attempts to deny that *we* or *our kind of people* could be implicated in the evil we find at work in others. A similarly negative evaluation could be made of one of the chief narratives that defined the world of the New Testament, a narrative of a different sort but equally at odds with a biblically formed interpretation of the march of history. For the Romans, what was old was regarded as far superior to what is recent or new, since over time the world, like the human body, is subject to deterioration, wear and tear. For the orator Dio Chrysostom (*ca.* 40/50–after 110 C.E.), to take one illustration, the world undoubtedly produced better things before it was worn out.[4] The world-story of the Bible is somewhat different, moving as it does from

---

[3]Francisco J. Ayala, "Human Nature: One Evolutionist's View," in *Whatever Happened to the Soul? Scientific and Theological Portraits of Human Nature*, ed. Warren S. Brown, Nancey Murphy, and H. Newton Malony, Theology and the Sciences (Minneapolis: Fortress Press, 1998), 31–48 (40–41); Warren S. Brown, "Cognitive Contributions to Soul," in *Whatever Happened to the Soul*, 99–125.
[4]Dio Chrysostom *Discourse* 31.75.

paradise to paradise lost to the possibility and hope of paradise regained.

Paradise, paradise lost: as unsophisticated as this plot summary may seem, it nonetheless centers our curiosity on the nature of what has been lost and what therefore needs to be recovered. In order to examine these key elements, we begin with the opening chapters of Genesis, to which generations have conveniently referred as the cycle of creation and fall. So significant is the portrait of humanity found here that, in the end, I will insist that salvation means nothing less, but nothing more, than our becoming fully and genuinely human.

Creation in the Image of God

What it means to "be saved," to be engaged in propagating and embodying the message of salvation, and to make one's way on the journey of salvation are all tied to the larger question, What does it mean to be human? And, of course, even the question, Do we need salvation? presumes an understanding of what it means to be human. What is our call or vocation, simply because we are members of the human family? More to the present point, what would a biblical account of our humanity look like?

Humanity in Contemporary Perspective

We should begin our investigation of this question by accounting for the challenges before us. On the one hand, it is simply the case that the writings of the Old and New Testament do not give us much in the way of a speculative account of the human person. Far more problematic, though, is that we already possess views of the human person, and these are often unacknowledged. For most of us, our answers to the question, What does it mean to be human? are little discussed, held implicitly, and therefore easily presumed to be based on or at least consistent with a biblical account. That is, it is easy to find in the Bible reflections of our own views, particularly if we are unaware that they are just that, *our own views.*

For this reason, it may be helpful to describe first how we have learned to construct what it means to be human. In his penetrating analysis of contemporary human identity in the West, philosopher Charles Taylor finds that personal identity has come to be based on presumed affirmations of the human subject as autonomous, disengaged, self-sufficient, and self-engaged. For Taylor, the development of this account of personal identity in the West can be traced from Augustine in the fourth to fifth centuries, through the major European philosophers of the seventeenth and eighteenth centuries (for example, Descartes, Locke, and Kant), into the present. What he finds is a "self defined by the powers of disengaged reason— with its associated ideals of self-responsible freedom and dignity—of self-exploration, and of personal commitment." These, especially the first two, provide a launching point for our modern conception of "inwardness." Modern identity is thus shaped by such assumptions as the following:

- Human dignity lies in self-sufficiency and self-determination.
- Identity is grasped in self-referential terms: I am who I am.
- Persons have an inner self, which is the authentic self.
- Basic to authentic personhood are self-autonomy and self-legislation.[5]

The upshot of this is a portrait of the human person that can be understood, as it were, one person at a time, with an individual's interior life of cardinal importance. Although Taylor does not focus much on the idea of a human "soul," it is nonetheless of interest that the view of human identity he sketches is one cultivated easily in the psychology that might arise from the garden of Plato or, more recently, Descartes. Taylor does identify the precondition for the modern emphasis on the human sense of the "authentic, inner person" in Plato's concept of the "soul" (*psychē*), however, and the Christian tradition has tended to agree. "Without the soul, we are nothing," wrote the African Christian apologist Tertullian in the early third century, "[Without the soul] there is not even the name of a human being— only that of a carcass" (3.532) . Personal identity has long been tied to the existence of an entity known as the soul, separate from the body, and identified with the person's highest and true "self."

The question is: Given this portrait of humanity, how might "salvation" be understood? Perhaps it is not surprising that contemporary soteriologies, drawn from such views of the human person as these, have tended to be oriented toward the personal decisions of individuals, and to a transformation of the "inner person."

---

[5]Charles Taylor, *Sources of the Self: The Making of the Modern Identity* (Cambridge, Mass.: Harvard Univ. Press, 1989), 211.

What is needed in this case is a "change of heart." Emphasis falls on a person's mastery of the soul over the body; one's capacity to enter into and enjoy a relationship with God is tied to the soul; and salvation of the soul is generally regarded as the means by which human identity can cross over the bridge between this life and the next. According to Francis Crick—who, together with James Watson, is responsible for deciphering the structure of DNA a half-century ago—these ideas are focused in a religious belief held today by billions of human beings.[6] As we shall now see, though, there is little about this portrait of the human person, or the soteriology that it funds, that is particularly biblical.

What Is Humanity?

With regard to the witness of scripture, our focus is fixed first on the following texts from Genesis 1—2:

> Then God said, "Let us make humankind in our image, according to our likeness; and let them have dominion over the fish of the sea, and over the birds of the air, and over the cattle, and over all the wild animals of the earth, and over every creeping thing that creeps upon the earth."
> So God created humankind in his image,
>   in the image of God he created them;
>   male and female he created them.
> God blessed them, and God said to them, "Be fruitful and multiply, and fill the earth and subdue it; and have dominion over the fish of the sea and over the birds of the air and over every living thing that moves upon the earth."...God saw everything that he had made, and indeed, it was very good. And there was evening and there was morning, the sixth day. (1:26–28, 31)

> These are the generations of the heavens and the earth when they were created.
> In the day that the LORD God made the earth and the heavens, when no plant of the field was yet in the earth and

[6]Francis Crick, *The Astonishing Hypothesis: The Scientific Search for the Soul* (New York: Simon & Schuster, 1994), 261.

no herb of the field had yet sprung up—for the LORD God had not caused it to rain upon the earth, and there was no one to till the ground; but a stream would rise from the earth, and water the whole face of the ground—then the LORD God formed man from the dust of the ground, and breathed into his nostrils the breath of life; and the man became a living being. And the LORD God planted a garden in Eden, in the east; and there he put the man whom he had formed. Out of the ground the LORD God made to grow every tree that is pleasant to the sight and good for food, the tree of life also in the midst of the garden, and the tree of the knowledge of good and evil... The LORD God took the man and put him in the garden of Eden to till it and keep it. And the LORD God commanded the man, "You may freely eat of every tree of the garden; but of the tree of the knowledge of good and evil you shall not eat, for in the day that you eat of it you shall die."

Then the LORD God said, "It is not good that the man should be alone; I will make him a helper as his partner." So out of the ground the LORD God formed every animal of the field and every bird of the air, and brought them to the man to see what he would call them; and whatever the man called every living creature, that was its name. The man gave names to all cattle, and to the birds of the air, and to every animal of the field; but for the man there was not found a helper as his partner. So the LORD God caused a deep sleep to fall upon the man, and he slept; then he took one of his ribs and closed up its place with flesh. And the rib that the LORD God had taken from the man he made into a woman and brought her to the man. Then the man said,

"This at last is bone of my bones
and flesh of my flesh;
this one shall be called Woman,
for out of Man this one was taken."

Therefore a man leaves his father and his mother and clings to his wife, and they become one flesh. And the man and his wife were both naked, and were not ashamed. (2:4–9, 15–25)

Two immediate affirmations derive from these texts, *continuity* and *difference*: the continuity of humanity with all other animals and, indeed, with the rest of creation; and the difference between humanity and other animals.

Generally speaking, Christians have been quick to grasp the latter, slow to recognize the former. We prefer to locate the human being in a place of incontestable honor at the center of the cosmos. Consequently, we have found ourselves humbled by scientific discovery—in the modern age, first by Copernicus, who demonstrated that our planet and, thus, we who inhabit the earth, are not the center around which the universe pivots; second, by Darwin and evolutionary biology, who located *homo sapiens* within the animal kingdom with a genetic make-up that strongly resembles the creatures around us (comparisons with chimpanzees at the DNA level indicate a similarity of about 98.4 percent); and most recently by neuroscience, with its tightening of the mind-brain link, which renders more and more improbable the need for the concept of the human soul as a separate entity capable of its own, independent existence.[7] As theologian Wolfhart Pannenberg has recognized, recent advances with regard to the close mutual interrelations of physical and psychological occurrences have raised serious questions in the face of traditional ideas of a soul distinct from the body that is detached from it in death. He inquires, "When the life of the soul is conditioned in every detail by bodily organs and processes, how can it be detached from the body and survive without it?"[8]

Humans, according to the biblical account of beginnings, are clearly like other living things in being created by God and thus in their relation to God. Like them, humanity is formed from the stuff of the earth. We may push further, noting that the Genesis narrative presents the sexes in a relationship of mutuality, parity, and egalitarianism. The male and female are created together and share the role of "filling the earth" and serving as its stewards. With the

[7]Helmut Thielicke lists "three humblings"—Copernicus, Darwin, and Freud — in *Being Human...Becoming Human: An Essay in Christian Anthropology* (Garden City, N.Y.: Doubleday, 1984), 29–32.

[8]Wolfhart Pannenberg, *Systematic Theology,* vol. 2 (Grand Rapids, Mich.: Wm.B. Eerdmans, 1994), 182. Pannenberg anticipated this position in his earlier works *What Is Man? Contemporary Anthropology in Theological Perspective* (Philadelphia: Fortress Press, 1970), 45–53; and *Anthropology in Theological Perspective* (Philadelphia: Westminster Press, 1985).

language of "partnering," the narrative provides no rationale for hierarchy or other differences of status or role. Not even the term "helper," used in reference to woman in Genesis 2:18, portends any notion of "subordination" or a servile role, since the term is used elsewhere in the Old Testament of God (for example, Gen. 49:25; Ex. 18:4). In the same way, the Genesis account says nothing that would provide for the human exploitation of nature. Vegetation is for both humans *and* animals (Gen. 1:30), and animals share with humans the command to reproduce, increase, and fill the seas and the earth (Gen. 1:22). The additional vocation given humanity, to "subdue" the earth and to "have dominion" over it (Gen. 1:26, 28), must be understood in the context of the order set forth in the creation account, a narrative in which there is no hint of either chaos or combat. True, the creation account imbues humanity with royal identity and task, but this is a nobility granted without conquest; its essence is realized in coexistence with all of life in the land, and in the cultivation of life. Similarly, Psalm 8:6 portrays humanity in a stance of dominion over creation, as though standing over its defeated enemies, but without hint of military action. Manage and care without conquest or domination—the human family has this responsibility in relation to God's creation because this is how God has made us.

Thus are humans *like* other living things, but also *unlike* them in being made in God's image. Of all the creatures mentioned in Genesis 1—2, only humanity is created after God's own likeness, in God's own image (*imago Dei*). Only to humanity does God speak directly. Humanity alone receives from God this divine vocation.

Humanity "in God's Image"

"So God created humankind in his image, in the image of God he created them" (Gen. 1:27). Whatever we might say about the relative succinctness of this text from Genesis, we should not confuse brevity with clarity! In fact, the *imago Dei* tradition has been the focus of diverse interpretations among Jews and Christians—ranging widely from some physical characteristic of humans (such as standing upright) to a way of knowing (especially the human capacity to know God), and so on. What is obvious is that humanity is thus defined in relation to God in terms of both similarity and difference: humanity is in some sense "like" God, but is itself not divine. Humanity thus stands in an ambivalent position—living in solidarity with the rest of the created order and yet distinct from it on account of humankind's unique role as the bearer of the divine image, called to a particular and crucial relationship with Yahweh and yet not divine.[9] Further interpretive steps can be taken. Taken within its immediate setting in Genesis 1, "the image of God" in which humanity is made is set in relation to the exercise of dominion over the earth on God's behalf. This observation does not take us far, however, since we must then ascertain what it means to exercise dominion in this way—that is, in a way that reflects God's own ways of interaction with God's creatures. What is more, this way of putting the issue does not grapple with the profound word spoken over humanity and about humanity, that human beings in themselves (and not merely in what they do) reflect the divine image. What is this quality that distinguishes humanity? God's words affirm the creation of the human family in its relation to God, as God's counterpart, so that the nature of humanity derives from the human family's relatedness to God. The concept of the *imago Dei*, then, is fundamentally relational, or covenantal, and takes as its ground and focus the graciousness of God's own covenantal relations with humanity and the rest of creation. The distinguishing mark of *human* existence when compared with other creatures is thus the whole of human existence (and not some "part" of the individual). Humanity is created uniquely in relationship to God and finds itself as a result of creation in covenant with God. Humanity is given the divine mandate to reflect God's own covenant love in relation with God, within the covenant community of all humanity, and with all that God has created.

Subsequent Christian theology has emphasized the triune nature of God—that is, the fundamental relatedness of God, three persons within the Godhead—from which all revelation flows and on the basis of which all creation exists and has its meaning. It would be easy to imagine that the community of the Godhead is replicated in a tripartite understanding of the human person—body, soul, and spirit. This would be a mistake in category. The human person, understood as an individual, is not a reflection of the Godhead, as though the

---

[9]Alister E. McGrath, *Scientific Theology,* vol. 1: *Nature* (Grand Rapids, Mich.: Wm. B. Eerdmans, 2001), 197. For a recent survey of ways in which creation of humanity "in the divine image" has been interpreted, together with a contemporary proposal, see Stanley J. Grenz, *The Social God and the Relational Self: A Trinitarian Theology of the Imago Dei,* The Matrix of Christian Theology (Louisville: Westminster John Knox Press, 2001).

human person were complete in her- or himself. God's words at the creation of humankind are spoken not over a human person, but over *adam*, the entire human family. In fact, according to Genesis, God (singular) created humanity (singular) as men and women (plural), as "them" (plural). In Christian terms, then, we reflect the community of the triune God not so much as individuals but as the human community, whose life is differentiated from and yet bound up with nature, and whose common life springs from and finds its end in God's embrace.

The Divine Image Elsewhere in Scripture

Outside of Genesis, creation "in the image of God" is hardly mentioned in the Old Testament, and on this basis it might be imagined that this concept has had or should have little influence in the faith of God's people. From the standpoint of a theological reading of the Bible as a whole, however, it is pivotal that we not underestimate the witness of Genesis 1. Study of narratives in general has emphasized the importance of beginnings for the way they establish the concerns, needs, and parameters within which the subsequent story might develop. Given this perspective, the creation of humanity in the divine image, and the recounting of this reality in the opening chapter of the Bible, is crucial, since it sets out for the whole of scripture, and for the whole of life, the cornerstone presupposition of all of our reflection on humanity. In ancient buildings the cornerstone was cut to a true 90-degree angle and was used to align the rest of the foundation stones to ensure that the building would be solidly built and would endure. To affirm the idea of the presence of the divine image in humankind as a "cornerstone presupposition," then, is to admit that this concept plays a determinative role in how humanity is to be measured. Indeed, it establishes at the outset of the biblical narrative the peculiar "need" for humans to realize their humanity as bearers of God's image. The being and doing of humans throughout scripture, and subsequently, is to be measured by this single canon. Creation for humanity thus entails gift and vocation, identity and call.

The nature of humanity is tied to the image of God also in Genesis 5:1–3; 9:5–6; Psalm 8, and in two New Testament texts, 1 Cor. 11:7; Jas. 3:9. Of these, the appearance of the idea in Genesis texts subsequent to the story of the fall of humanity in Genesis 3 is of special importance, since these certify that the disobedience of Adam and Eve does not disinherit the rest of humanity from its defining quality, "created in the divine image." Also of real interest is the text in James, where the writer seems to shake his head in disbelief at the way we use our tongues: "With it we bless the Lord and Father, and with it we curse those who are made in the likeness of God." It is not only that this text suggests the degree to which the identity of humanity as bearers of the divine image lies in the background of biblical faith more generally. Nor is it only that this text thus draws a straight line from our actions toward one another to our behavior toward God. Together with the witness of Genesis 1, this text also reminds us that creation in the image of God is a theological statement about the whole of humanity—and not only regarding those who lived "in the beginning," nor narrowly defined as those who would later be called out as God's people. Inside and outside Israel, and the church, we encounter people, all of whom "are made in the likeness of God."

The language of "the image of God" is also used of humanity in other Jewish texts from the centuries around the time of Christ, and preeminently of Jesus in the New Testament. In the New Testament, Paul's thought is closest to the interpretation of the *imago Dei* expressed in the first-century Jewish writing known as the Wisdom of Solomon, wherein the phrase is used with reference to the actual expression of the "image of God" in a human life rather than to human capacity or potential. Paul develops the motif of Christ as the "image of God" (2 Cor. 4:4; Col. 1:15; compare Phil. 2:6) and, as its corollary, the conformation of human beings into the image of Christ (Rom. 8:29; 1 Cor. 15:49; 2 Cor. 3:18). One might say on this basis that christology is first anthropology, that we have in Christ the measure of authentic personhood.

What of "the Soul"?

The affirmation of human beings as bearers of the divine image in Genesis, together with the interpretation of the *imago Dei* tradition at the hands of Paul, points unquestionably to the uniqueness of humanity in comparison to all other creatures. This tradition does not locate this singularity in the human possession of a "soul," but in the human capacity to relate to Yahweh as covenant partner, and to join in companionship within the human family and in relation to the whole cosmos in ways that reflect the covenant love of God. Indeed, within the Old Testament, "soul" (*nephesh*) refers to life and vitality—not life in general, but as instantiated in human persons and animals;

not a thing to have but a way to be. To speak of loving God with all of one's "soul" (for example, Deut. 6:5), then, is to elevate the intensity of involvement of the entirety of one's being.

What, then, of Genesis 2:7 (in my own translation: "the Lord God formed the human being of the dust of the ground, breathed into his nostrils the breath of life, and the human being became a living soul [*nephesh*])"? The term in question, *nephesh*, is used only a few verses earlier with reference to "every beast of the earth," "every bird of the air," and "everything that creeps on the earth"—that is, to everything "in which there is life (*nephesh*)" (1:30; my translation). This demonstrates that "soul" is not for the Genesis story a unique characteristic of the human person. Accordingly, one might better translate Genesis 2:7 with reference to the divine gift of *life*: "the human being became fully alive" (my translation). In this way, Genesis does not define humanity in essentialist terms but in relational—more specifically identifying the human person as Yahweh's partner, and with emphasis on the communal, intersexual character of personhood, the quality of care the human family is to exercise with regard to creation as God's representative, the importance of the human modeling of the personal character of God, and the unassailable vocation of humans to reflect in their relationships God's own character.[10]

Painting the Human Person

Were we to summarize what we have found in the Genesis story of humanity's origins, and add to it those emphases that develop more fully in the Old and New Testaments as a whole, we would find a portrait of humanity that is quite at odds with those notions that define humankind in the contemporary West. Recall the qualities that Charles Taylor identified in his exploration of *Sources of the Self*, emphasizing the human subject as autonomous, self-legislating, self-sufficient, and self-engaged. An analysis of the portrayal of humanity found in scripture includes such emphases as the following:

---

[10]See further, Walter Brueggemann, *Theology of the Old Testament: Testimony, Dispute, Advocacy* (Minneapolis: Fortress Press, 1997), 451–52; Colin E. Gunton, "Trinity, Ontology and Anthropology: Towards a Renewal of the Doctrine of the *Imago Dei*," in *Persons Divine and Human: King's College Essays on Theological Anthropology*, ed. Christoph Schwöbel and Colin E. Gunton (Edinburgh: T. & T. Clark, 1991), 47–61; Christoph Schwöbel, "Human Being as Relational Being: Twelve Theses for a Christian Anthropology," in *Persons Divine and Human*, 141–70.

- the construction of the self as ineluctably nested in social relationships and, then, the importance of relational interdependence for human life and identity
- a premium on the health and integrity of the human community
- the assumption that a person *is* one's behavior—that is, that one's deepest commitments are unavoidably exhibited in one's practices—so that attention focuses on "embodied life," disallowing the possibility that the "real" person might be relegated to one's interior life
- the call to live out the human vocation as this is drawn from a vision of Yahweh's own character, God's "difference" (or holiness) in relation to the cosmos[11]

If human beings were to reject their identity as humans, their vocation to be human, expressed in these terms, and thus be found in need of restoration to their true selves, what would this salvation look like? What soteriology might result? We may recall that, given contemporary views of the human person in the West, emphasis falls on a person's mastery of the soul over the body; one's capacity to enter into and enjoy a relationship with God is tied to the individual's interior life; and salvation of a person's "inner essence" is generally regarded as the means by which human identity can cross over the bridge between this life and the next. Over against this soteriology, biblical portraits of human nature point toward restoration to covenantal relationship to God, recovery of human community in its vitality, and the reintegration of one's self as a person fully embodied in relation to others and to the world in which life with and before God might be lived.

Again, such a soteriology would arise *if* humanity were to reject the gift of its peculiarity as bearers of the divine image and its call to be fully human. What happens as we turn the page in the narrative of human beginnings in Genesis?

The "Fall" and the Human Situation

Within the good order of creation, God had carved out a space for Adam, a garden within which "God made to grow every tree that

---

[11]Robert A. Di Vito has analyzed this material for the Old Testament, but many of his observations are equally apropos of such New Testament materials as Matthew, Luke-Acts, or James, to name only a few representatives ("Old Testament Anthropology and the Construction of Personal Identity," *Catholic Biblical Quarterly* 61 [1999]: 217–38).

is pleasant to the sight and good for food." Here, too, grew the tree of life and the tree of the knowledge of good and evil (Gen. 2:8–9). This is the garden from which, by the end of Genesis 3, the man and woman will have been expelled. The chain of encounters leading to expulsion has attracted interpretations of all kinds, from theologically laden analyses of "The Fall" to Sigmund Freud's assessment that the latent content of Genesis 3 concerns an adolescent's erotic attachment to his mother's affections (i.e., the Oedipus complex).[12] Our interest falls on the ramifications of this account for the unfolding story of humanity and its significance for the journey of salvation.

Garden, Humanity, and Serpent

Genesis 3 opens as follows:

> Now the serpent was more crafty than any other wild animal that the LORD God had made. He said to the woman, "Did God say, 'You shall not eat from any tree in the garden'?" The woman said to the serpent, "We may eat of the fruit of the trees in the garden; but God said, 'You shall not eat of the fruit of the tree that is in the middle of the garden, nor shall you touch it, or you shall die.'" But the serpent said to the woman, "You will not die; for God knows that when you eat of it your eyes will be opened, and you will be like God, knowing good and evil." So when the woman saw that the tree was good for food, and that it was a delight to the eyes, and that the tree was to be desired to make one wise, she took of its fruit and ate; and she also gave some to her husband, who was with her, and he ate. Then the eyes of both were opened, and they knew that they were naked; and they sewed fig leaves together and made loincloths for themselves.
>
> They heard the sound of the LORD God walking in the garden at the time of the evening breeze, and the man and his wife hid themselves from the presence of the LORD God among the trees of the garden. But the LORD God called to the man, and said to him, "Where are you?" (Gen. 3:1–9)

---

[12]Genesis 3 has been the object of a wide range of psychological analyses, and these are perceptively surveyed and assessed in D. Andrew Kille, *Psychological Biblical Criticism*, Guides to Biblical Scholarship: Old Testament Series (Minneapolis: Fortress Press, 2001).

The terms of the temptation faced by the woman in the garden are startling. First, in representing God as forbidding the consumption of any of the garden's fruit, the serpent engages in a ridiculous exaggeration. If they could not eat, how could they survive? Second, the serpent proposes that partaking of a particular tree will transpose humans into being "like God." Yet, humankind is already "like God," being bearers of the divine image. This strongly suggests that the serpent has put forward an alternative, and misleading, concept of God. Indeed, the very presence of the serpent, one of the beasts (Gen. 2:19–20), in the garden, a place of ordered, domesticated habitation, together with his opening characterization as one who engages in premeditated scheming (Gen. 3:1), ensures our hearing his claims as ill-formed, deceptive, out of place. Third, what the woman sees is a tree "good for food," "a delight to the eyes," "to be desired to make one wise" (Gen. 3:6), yet the man and woman already inhabit a world surrounded by every tree that was "pleasant to the sight and good for food" (Gen. 2:9). Given these three observations, what comes into special focus is the serpent's two-pronged portrayal of the character of God and of what it means "to be like God": "your eyes will be opened, and you will be like God, knowing good and evil" (Gen. 3:5). Again, it may be startling to discover that the words spoken by the serpent are true at least in some significant sense; having eaten of the fruit of the forbidden tree, their eyes are indeed opened (Gen. 3:7), just as the serpent foretold.

It is precisely here that things begin to go awry, for the knowledge promised by the serpent and desired by the man and woman is not that wisdom that resides in life before Yahweh. Rather than becoming gods, the man and woman become aware of their nakedness—a condition signifying in the biblical and later Jewish traditions the gravest dishonor. (See 2 Sam. 6:20.) Clearly, being "like God," in the sense promised by the serpent, was not what it was anticipated to be.

The serpent had proposed to the woman the arbitrariness of God's prohibition regarding the tree in the middle of the garden, and this leads the woman and the man to the judgment that the life set before them by Yahweh was in fact deficient in some significant sense. Partaking of the fruit, they would begin their apotheosis, their heavenly journey, their divinization. At its center, the temptation they faced and into which they entered was a denial of their creaturely status before God, the gift of their nobility within creation and the vocation to be humanity in dependence on God. The ensuing narrative is overtaken with references in the first-person, "I," documenting a tragic crescendo of self-aggrandizement, self-legislation, self-orientation, and self-dependence. The fruit, so appealing in prospect, is transformed into bitter disappointment. With their newfound enlightenment, they are newly introduced to a need they had not previously known, their need for a covering for their nakedness, their shame, their vulnerability.

Genesis 3 introduces into the biblical narrative no particular vocabulary of sin, such as "disobedience" or "transgression" or "to do evil," but the concept of sin is very much on display. Sin is portrayed as the use of God's good gift of freedom of decision, to decide against God. Old Testament theologian H. D. Preuss adds that sin is here "understood as the failure to recognize the authority of God and as preferring to discuss the divine word rather than observe it"—perhaps to deflect its applicability to themselves or to question whether it is fair or good. Such behavior is the denial of human responsibility to God, the willful attempt for humans to make themselves lord of their own lives.[13]

Sin, the Human Epidemic

What are the outcomes of this misrepresentation of the divine command, this disobedience to Yahweh, this denial of the place of the human in the cosmos? Like watching a series of dominoes fall, one after the other, so the text sketches a series of consequences. First, sin proves to be contagious, with sin leading to sin, from one sinner to the next (Gen. 3:6). The human couple learn shame and vulnerability, leading not to efforts at reconciliation with God for their disobedience but to further alienation, even to the point of hiding from Yahweh's presence. In Psalm 8, God's attention to the human family is astonishing but welcome. To humanity in the garden, however, Yahweh's voice has become a menace. Refusing to heed Yahweh directing humanity not to eat of that tree (Gen. 2:17), they now hear that voice differently, not as an invitation to relationship but as a threat. Moreover, the woman and man both learn to deflect responsibility—the man blaming the woman, the woman the serpent—as they embrace the role of victim. Alienation extends, then,

---

[13]Horst Dietrich Preuss, *Old Testament Theology*, 2 vols, Old Testament Library (Louisville: Westminster John Knox Press, 1996) 2:171.

from the human-divine relationship to all forms of relatedness, between persons and between humankind and the cosmos. Given a liberal dose of freedom to organize the world in relation to God's creatures, humanity nonetheless has before it a vocation before God, the divine will rather than self-procured wisdom, and moral responsibility. Human self-determination leads now to a freedom that exceeds its grasp and a harmony set aside in favor of struggle, hierarchy, drudgery.[14]

What is lost in the Garden, then, is the humanness of humanity—that is, the fullness of what it means genuinely to be human in the context of the ordered creation within and in relation to which God has formed the human creature. As a result, in a very real (though perhaps unexpected) sense, the woman's prediction, that partaking of the fruit of the forbidden tree would result in death (Gen. 3:3), was realized. This is because, in the scriptures of Israel, death is never a phenomenon focused merely on biological cessation, but especially the severance of all relationships—relationships with God and with every person and with everything in the cosmos. This is why Ray Anderson can helpfully observe that "death is a threat to personhood, not merely a fact of natural life."[15] Even Sheol, the place of the dead, is only very rarely deployed in the Old Testament as the common location of the dead. Rather, in most instances the term is used with reference to that fate to which the ungodly are consigned and to which the godly declare their aversion. It is the antithesis of heaven. That is, the subterranean world of the dead is associated especially with the wicked, underscoring the Old Testament distinction between life (lived in this world, before and in relation to Yahweh) and death (assigned to the underworld, separate from Yahweh).[16]

Genesis 3 is only the beginning, however. The narrative goes on to enumerate one episode of sin and alienation after another: Cain's

---

[14]William P. Brown, *The Ethos of the Cosmos: The Genesis of Moral Imagination in the Bible* (Grand Rapids, Mich.: Wm. B. Eerdmans, 1999), 160–61.

[15]Ray S. Anderson, *Theology, Death and Dying* (London: Basil Blackwell, 1986), 46. Cf. John Goldingay, "Death and Afterlife in the Psalms," in *Judaism in Late Antiquity*, part 4: *Death, Life-after-Death, Resurrection and the World-to-Come in the Judaisms of Antiquity*, ed. Alan J. Avery-Peck and Jacob Neusner, Handbook of Oriental Studies—1: The Near and Middle East 49 (Leiden: E. J. Brill, 2000), 61–85; Roland E. Murphy, "Death and Afterlife in the Wisdom Literature," in *Death, Life-after-Death, Resurrection, and the World-to-Come*, 101–16.

[16]Cf. e.g., Pss. 9:18; 16:10; 30:4; 31:18; 49:16; 55:16; 86:13; 88:6; Isa. 5:14; Job 24:19; also Desmond Alexander, "The Old Testament View of Life after Death," *Themelios* 11 (1986): 41–46 (43–44); Philip Johnston, "The Underworld and the Dead in the Old Testament," *Tyndale Bulletin* 45 (1994): 415–19 (416).

murderous act results in his exile (Gen. 4:1–16); a restless, godless society emerges (Gen. 4:17–24; 5:28–29); global violence leads to global destruction (Gen. 6:1—9:18); sin even among Noah's family leads to the enslavement of one people by another (Gen. 9:17–27); and, finally, the imperialism of conquest, leading to a tower made to reach the heavens, leads to the confusion of languages (Gen. 11).[17] Sin even of this magnitude cannot irreparably mar the divine purpose in creation, however. Even the words of God spoken to a rebellious humanity on the plains of Shinar, construction zone for the infamous Tower of Babel, are nothing less than a reiteration of Yahweh's words in creation, to multiply and spread throughout the whole earth (Gen. 1:28; 9:7; 11:6–9). Here in the opening chapters of Genesis, therefore, we find the basic contours of the ongoing saga: God acts and speaks; humanity refuses its vocation, responds in disobedience, and experiences the consequences of its sin; God extends the offer of relationship again in forgiveness and reconciliation.

Tracing the story from Genesis into the rest of Israel's scriptures, we discover sin to be a characteristic feature of human existence. This is not because of the hereditary quality of sin, nor is there yet the sort of view that we will later find in Paul, that all humanity has somehow participated in the sin of the first human being. In fact, the origin of sin is not a typical source of speculation, though there is occasional reference to the fountainhead of human weakness (for example, Job 4:20; 25:6; Pss. 78:38–39; 103:13–14). More common is the rehearsal of those simple words associated with David's own confession, following his transgression of the law against adultery: "I have sinned" (2 Sam. 12:13);[18] or by the people at signal points of turning back to God: "We have sinned."[19] New Testament witnesses agree with this emphasis on the universality of sin. "All have sinned and fall short of the glory of God" (Rom. 3:23), Paul writes, and, according to the Gospels of Matthew and Luke, Jesus teaches his followers, all of them, to pray for forgiveness of sins (Mt. 6:12; Lk. 11:4). Given the breadth of the notion of "conversion" in the ancient Roman world, to signal a moving deeper into one's own religion as well as to embrace a new

---

[17]See Robin C. Cover, "Sin, Sinners (Old Testament)," in *Anchor Bible Dictionary*, 6 vols., ed. David Noel Freeman (New York: Doubleday, 1992) 6:31–40 (38).

[18]E.g., Josh. 7:20; 1 Sam. 15:24; 2 Sam. 12:13; 19:21; 24:10; Pss. 41:5; 51:6; et al.

[19]E.g., Num. 14:40; 21:7; Judg. 10:10, 15; 1 Sam. 7:6; 12:10; 1 Kings 8:47; et al.

religion,[20] the universality of sin is highlighted, too, by the call to repentance, set before Jews and Gentiles alike in the missionary preaching of Acts (for example, Acts 2:38; 17:30).

For Paul, as for scripture as a whole, the condition of humanity is not exhausted by descriptions of weakness or frailty. Sin reaches further, with images of transgression, rebellion, failure.[21] For the letter of James, to take one example, the human condition is sketched in terms of double-mindedness, a lack of integrity: friends of God or friends of the world? (See Jas. 1:27; 2:5, 23; 4:4.) Double-mindedness is tied to desire, which entices persons to evil. Evil boils up from hell (Jas. 3:6), but is not experienced by persons as an alien presence; rather, we find within ourselves a raging battle of desire (Jas. 1:13–14; 4:1–4). The half-hearted are characterized by doubt, instability, and wavering, whereas those wholly devoted to God enjoy stability, faith, and caring community.

Turning to Paul, it is especially in his letter to the Romans that the apostle reflects on the nature of sin. It simply "entered the world" (Rom. 5:12, author's translation), "came to life" (Rom. 7:14, author's translation), and now enslaves not only individuals but, indeed, all of humanity (Rom. 1:18–32; 3:23). The concept of enslavement to sin is important for Paul. (See Rom. 5:12—8:3, and especially Rom. 6:16–23.) "Sin" is a power that can lord it over a person (Rom. 6:12, 14), a master to which one must pay wages (Rom. 6:23), an owner to which people have been sold in the slave market (Rom. 7:14).

Freedom and the Mastery of Sin

Does portraying "sin" in almost personal terms as a taskmaster negate human choice and culpability? Since Paul regards human beings as responsible for their behavior, his position acknowledges the human freedom to choose. Sin remains an option, a road that need not be taken. But what sort of choice is this? If the human family, globally and historically, has embraced sin and consequently has been given over by God to further sin (Rom. 1:18–32), what range of options remains genuinely open to us? If the values and practices honored in the universe of our lives, the ideals and modes of conduct that characterize its systems and institutions, are set in opposition to the

[20]See chapter 4: "How Can We Be Saved?"
[21]See G. B. Caird and L. D. Hurst, *New Testament Theology* (Oxford: Oxford Univ. Press, 1994) 74–117.

ways of God,[22] then the pull of sin's gravity is difficult to escape indeed. Genuine choice can come only in the context of authentic options, and this highlights the importance for Paul of proclamation and community. Another vision of the world is needed, one that reminds us that rebellion in Eden may be our common heritage but not necessarily our defining influence. Here, we are invited to community life oriented toward resisting evil and sin and to practices of faith, hope, and love that remind both church and world that we were created for more than this.

For Paul, then, sin is a refusal to acknowledge one's creaturely status before God, a refusal to glorify God as God, on display in Adam's refusal to heed God's prohibition to self-indulgence in the garden (Rom. 1:18–32). Pursuing wisdom apart from God, knowledge apart from life, humans exchange creature for creator, engage in idolatry, and journey down a road that leads to a form of existence that can only be labeled as "subhuman." Again, this is an important point, for it is easy today to imagine that participation in sin is a natural part of our lives. "We are only human," after all. Long ago, however, Tertullian observed the oxymoron in the idea of "natural sinfulness": "The corruption of nature is another nature."[23] Sinful humanity is human nature "reversed."[24] Even when sin seems our natural companion, sinfulness is actually a denial of that humanity in which we were formed and to which we are called.

At the same time, our experience is that sinfulness is inherent to our self-awareness and seems to flow out of "the way the world is." Here we look into the mirror of the paradox of our humanity. Here we see God's pronouncement over our creation that humanity is "very good," imbued with the vocation of nobility in relation to the cosmos. And yet there is also the sobering recognition of our limits and proclivity to expressions of evil, socially and personally. Reflecting on his own rise to power as an officer in the Soviet army, Aleksandr Solzhenitsyn wrote, "Pride grows in the human heart like lard on a pig"—this, as he came to realize that the demonic "system" that robbed him of so much of his life, that left him cruelly imprisoned, was not

---

[22]See, for example, 1 Cor. 1:26–29; 3:18–19; 4:9–13; 5:9–11, and so forth.
[23]Tertullian De anima, 41.
[24]So Werner Georg Kümmel, Man in the New Testament (London: Epworth, 1963), 87.

an invention of Soviet Russia but the progeny of the human heart.[25] And yet the witness of the Genesis text also embraces humanity in God's own work of creation and caring. Just because Adam and Eve were expelled from the garden does not mean that the garden should not continue to help define our reason for being, our vocation, the world toward which we orient our lives. We were made for more than this.

Yet, this is not often our experience. We easily find ourselves on a staircase spiraling downward from one landing to the next, with each controlled by another expression of sin's mastery in our lives. Theologian Ted Peters names seven of these.[26] The first is *anxiety*, the fear of loss and especially the fear of losing ourselves, ultimately in death. We experience anxiety as the "sting of death" in our lives, and combat it with illusions of immortality. We want to deny death—that is, to deny that we have limitations, that our abilities and even our existence has boundaries. The temptation to "be like God" is rooted here, in our unwillingness simply and fully to be human, to be creatures whose lives are finite and dependent on God.

The second is *unfaith*, the failure to trust. Failing to trust God, we refuse to live in God's care and assume we must care for ourselves. We find that we are unable to trust our neighbors, whose own existence is troublesome to us, not least when their lives interrupt our own or when their success or failures threaten us. We are the gods in control of our own lives, and we mirror in our lives the whims of the mythical gods of old who manipulate people and events to our own ends.

The third is *pride*, where our tendencies toward the divine come to the surface, when our "me," "my," and "mine" occupy center stage. This might be manifested in heightened self-control, in *machismo*, in prejudice, but also in refusing the social spotlight and in playing the role of the victim. Peters observes that characteristic of the proud is the capacity to ignore the suffering and needs of others—whether those others are outside of myself or even belong to another group or nation. National, ethnic, or even religious pride are possible manifestations of sin.

---

[25]Aleksandr I. Solzhenitsyn, *The Gulag Archipelago: 1918–1956* (London: Book Club, 1974), 163.

[26]Ted Peters, *Sin: Radical Evil in Soul and Society* (Grand Rapids, Mich.: Wm. B. Eerdmans, 1994). On what follows, see also David Atkinson, "What Difference Does the Cross Make to Life?" in *Atonement Today: A Symposium at St. John's College, Nottingham*, ed. John Goldingay (London: S.P.C.K., 1995), 253–71.

The fourth is the *desire to possess*, and includes desire, lust, envy, greed, and coveting. The desire to possess is also a group or national phenomenon as well as an individual one, and is the false solution to the sinful need to shore up one's own resources and to pretend that one is self-sufficient. Sin parades as self-promotion, self-provision, self-determination, and self-perpetuation.

Fifth, pride and the desire to possess lead to *self-justification*, which is nothing less than the desire to possess what only God possesses—namely, goodness. We turn to the mirror to define what is right and what is good. The measuring stick is my life. Those who do not measure up must be cut down (whether in gossip, slander, or some other form of violence) for there is nothing that makes us look so good as the failure or losses of others. Even God becomes susceptible to the implications of our self-justification: Having established the benchmark for what is good, we castigate God for not measuring up. Having established the correct definition of loving, we wonder why God can be so unloving. Having established the correct definition of justice, we presume God's work must conform to this standard. Self-justification is self-delusionment, a lie about ourselves that we embrace and which gives us license to speak violent words and do violent acts against those who are not "us," and who therefore do not measure up.

Sixth, then, is genuine *cruelty*, where those who have no empathy for those in pain actually inflict pain—whether physical or social or emotional or spiritual, whether to humans or to other creatures. Is this not the work of a god, wielding the power of life and death over others?

Finally, sin is *blasphemy*, the use of God and the things of God in self-justification. The holy writings support our position and our actions, we say. God has commanded us to kill, we allege. "Who are you to question a servant of God?" we ask. The word of the cross, which calls into question all pretensions to power and status, is replaced with our own words. Nothing—not the scriptures, not the church, not the Holy Spirit—nothing can call us into question, just as nothing can give hope to those who suffer under our behavior, since we have drafted God to our own ends.

This catalog is helpful for its focus on human motivations and allegiances, even if we might want to explore the relation of these images to others, such as sin-as-idolatry. In fact, the Old and New Testaments contain an abundance of terms and phrases for conceiving the condition that characterizes our lives: slavery, hard-heartedness, lostness, friendship with the world, ungodliness, wickedness, unrighteousness, living according to the sinful nature, the reprobate mind, the darkened heart, lacking worship, enemies of God, dead in one's trespasses and sins, children of (the first) Adam, lacking the glory of God, and more. In these and other ways, the human condition is assessed in scripture. Sin obviously comes in many guises! In part, this is because people at different times of social and psychological development manifest and experience sin in different ways. It is also due to the reality that people dwell in different social environments, with some terms and phrases more appropriate in this environment than in another.

This catalog has its limitations, too, since it construes sin primarily in terms of self-promotion or self-assertion. In recent decades, a number of theologians have observed that sin can just as easily be manifest in marginalized persons and communities. Sin might take the form of a numbing of the self rather than self-assertion, or a failure to embrace one's personhood rather than a predisposition to extend it at the expense of others. Manipulation of others and other coercive behavior, moreover, can be performed by those who seem to be powerless as well as those whose power is more visible and muscular. Seen in this way, "pride," for example, is more pervasive among humans than its popular identification with *machismo* or conceit might suggest. Although sin might be expressed as *machismo*, it also has its shadowy sides, as persons at all points of the continuum of power and privilege refuse to embrace either *only* or *fully* their places as full members within the human family.

We see more clearly from this way of putting the matter that "acts of disobedience" are deeply rooted in the sick soil of widely held convictions about the nature of our humanity that run counter to those of God. It is in this important sense that we recognize that sin was there even before we sinned. Our actions do not introduce evil into the world. Sin arrived before we did. Its power surrounds us and draws us into itself.

This reality does not spell the loss of our freedom to choose, but it does suggest the degree to which our choices are circumscribed already by the worlds in which we live. Contrary to the claims of the serpent in the garden, the concepts of good and evil do not exist in a vacuum. These are not "objective" realities, but must be understood in relation to some instrument of measuring. Living in a world that measures "the good" always in relation to "my" interests or the interests of "my group" or of "people like me" presses upon us choices that perpetuate disobedience, estrangement, disharmony, alienation. What of "the good" as defined by God's own words spoken over creation? Like those who live with lifelong disease, we have adjusted our existence to account for our maladies. We can scarcely imagine what the freedom to choose God's "good" would be, so much have we adapted ourselves to estrangement and alienation. We are in need of the medicine of liberation. We need salvation. We need a savior.

Epilogue

The first word was God's, as was the second. The first was creative, the second evaluative. Surveying the horizons of the cosmos, inspecting the living creatures raised up from the ground, God saw that it was "good." Surveying God's work on the day of humanity's appearance, God's word was "very good." But these are not the only words spoken, and we are not far into the Genesis story before God's stature and authority are under evaluation by those into whom God breathed life. Found wanting in the human grasp for self-authorization and self-rule, God's ways are renegotiated, set aside. So began the miserable procession from sin to sin, with the whole human family implicated in clearing its own path, a way marked by disobedience and alienation, by sin. Offered and accepted as a path to enlightenment, it turns perversely into the wilderness. Thankfully, the last word has not yet been spoken.

2

YAHWEH, THE HEALER

Perhaps the most enduring series of portraits of Jesus places him in any number of poses, with hand outstretched to touch the sick with the power of divine healing: Jesus the healer. Such images are among the most memorable and pervasive in the gospels. Together, the writings of Matthew, Mark, and Luke contain dozens of healing stories, including the raising of the crippled, the cleansing of lepers, exorcism for the demonized, recovery of sight to the blind, raising up the dead, and more.

What has this to do with the biblical theme of salvation? This is a thoroughly modern question, one that would not likely have occurred to most of Jesus' day. If in the last three centuries we in the West have learned to drive a wedge between the craft (and, more recently, the business) of healing on the one hand, salvation on the other, we ought not imagine that such distinctions would have come easily to inhabitants of either ancient Israel or the first-century Roman world. Rather, we should consider the following:

- Scripture as a whole presumes the intertwining of salvation and healing.

- Scripture as a whole interprets the image of Yahweh the savior as Yahweh the healer, and the New Testament adds to this the portrait of Jesus as God's agent of healing.
- The larger Roman world of Jesus' day conceived of salvation as healing.
- God's people are called to be a community of healing and health.

These realities underscore the need to consider how salvation and healing are related, and to examine particularly the biblical presentation of Yahweh the healer.

Salvation is an enormously wide-ranging concept in the biblical materials, and the biblical writers use a diverse assortment of terms to give it particular focus. In this chapter and the next, I want to explore two broad ways in which scripture portrays Yahweh as savior—in this chapter, Yahweh the healer; in the next, Yahweh the liberator. Although these two images may appear to stand in opposition, it is important to realize that the biblical witness finds no difficulty here. In fact, biblical writers can refer to the identical saving act of Yahweh at one point with the language of liberation, at another with the language of healing. Attending to these two portraits will allow us to come face to face with the same God and the same saving work of this God, albeit from different perspectives and with different emphases. It will also allow us to sketch some of the other, related ways in which salvation is represented in the scriptures, such as reconciliation, justification, "new creation," and forgiveness. We begin, then, with salvation as healing, and with the pervasiveness and profundity of the image of Yahweh the healer in Israel's scriptures.

Salvation as Healing: Setting the Context

In the New Testament world, the Greek terms associated with "salvation"—*sōzō* ("to save"), *sōtēr* ("savior"), *sōtērion* ("saving"), and *sōtēria* ("salvation")—related generally to rescue from misfortune of all kinds: shipwreck, the ravages of a journey, enemies in times of conflict, and so on. By far, however, the most common usage of these terms in the larger Greco-Roman world was medical. "To save" was "to heal." People might even refer to their physicians as "saviors." People other than physicians, who contributed to the welfare of a city, for example, could also be thought of as bringing salvation.

How distant the world of Jesus and Paul is from many of our presumptions can be underscored here. Miracles of healing in the Roman Mediterranean region were claimed by and for "holy men." We might expect this, but be caught off guard by evidence that miracles of healing were also attributed to kings, emperors, and military leaders. Here is solid testimony that "salvation" cannot be relegated to the sphere of the ethereal, as though it were concerned merely with "things of the spirit" or especially otherworldly in its focus. Deliverance from the enemy was as much a political statement as a spiritual one (or as much a spiritual as a political one), so that recovery of health in the case of an individual or a people could be cataloged as "salvation," "rescue," "peace," or "healing." This merging of hopes is well illustrated in a text written by the Alexandrian Jew Philo, *The Embassy to Gaius*, concerning the Emperor (or Caesar) Augustus (63 B.C.E.–14 C.E.):

And again the great regions which divide the inhabited world, Europe and Asia, were contending with each other for sovereign power...so that the whole human race exhausted by mutual slaughter was on the verge of utter destruction, had it not been for one man and leader, Augustus whom men fitly call the averter of evil. This is the Caesar who calmed the torrential storms on every side, who healed pestilences common to Greeks and barbarians, pestilences which descending from the south and east coursed to the west and north sowing seeds of calamity over the places and waters which lay between them.[1]

Philosophers, too, could be spoken of as though they were "physicians," whose teaching was to heal the vices of their auditors and to promote the good health of virtue. In fact, Galen (129–?199/216 C.E.), the celebrated physician whose medical theories and practices dominated from the second century C.E. into the seventeenth century, entitled one of his books *That the Best Physician Is also a Philosopher*. Continuing the metaphor, a philosopher might call for a change of diet and medicine, or even the surgical knife or hot iron to cauterize a wound. Corruption of inner character demanded radical intervention! The Roman philosopher Seneca (first century C.E.) says of

[1]Philo, *The Embassy to Gaius* §§ 144–45 (English translation in *Philo*, 10 vols. [Cambridge, Massachusetts: Harvard Univ. Press, 1962] 10:73–74).

himself, "I myself am to be cauterized, operated upon, or put on a diet."[2]

Of course, in the Greco-Roman world, healing could refer more narrowly to physical restoration, and in such cases healing was one of the benefits of salvation. Among the deities, Hercules, Asclepius, and Isis were particularly known for their healing ministrations. Though exalted from mortal existence to the Greek pantheon, Hercules remained compassionate toward humanity and acted on their behalf to heal diseases of all sorts, including raising the dead. The goddess Isis was well-known for her healing, and was recognized as queen of the universe, dispenser of life, healer, and bringer of salvation. Devotees of Asclepius labeled their god "Savior." He was the god of healing, who, it was presumed, guided the hands of the physicians. *Hygeia*, personified health, was said to be his daughter.

Acts of healing were not limited to the gods. Indeed, worship of Jesus as Lord was challenged in the Roman world by the ever-expanding worship of the emperor. As we saw in the case of Augustus, Rome's emperors could be recognized as bringing salvation (health, prosperity, peace, security) to the known world. Their saving work was regarded as proof of their enjoying the blessings and support of the gods, so that, again, religion and politics become mutually informing and supportive of one another. Tacitus (?56–?118 C.E.), the Latin historian, credits Vespasian (9–79 C.E.) with acts of healing; these were interpreted by the emperor and, perhaps more importantly, by the masses, as demonstrations of the lofty esteem in which Vespasian was held by the gods.[3]

Such usage would not have been alien to the scriptures of Israel, available in Greek translation from the third and second centuries B.C.E. onward, where the language of "salvation" might refer to deliverance, healing, health, and prosperity. Sometimes the connection is explicit, as in this prophetic word of Jeremiah:

> O hope of Israel! O LORD!
> All who forsake you shall be put to shame;

---

[2]Seneca *Epistulae morales*, 75:6–7.

[3]Related material is conveniently collected in Wendy Cotter, *Miracles in Greco-Roman Antiquity: A Sourcebook* (London: Routledge, 1999), 11–53. More generally, see Ceslas Spicq, *Theological Lexicon of the New Testament*, 3 vols (Peabody, Mass.: Hendrickson, 1994) 3:344–49.

those who turn away from you shall be recorded in the
    underworld,
  for they have forsaken the fountain of living water,
    the LORD.
Heal me, O LORD, and I shall be healed;
  save me, and I shall be saved;
    for you are my praise. (Jer. 17:13–14).

Like water to the thirsty (Isa. 12:3), salvation addresses the threat
of sin (Isa. 64:5) and sickness. Says Yahweh,

For the hurt of my poor people I am hurt,
  I mourn, and dismay has taken hold of me.
Is there no balm in Gilead?
  Is there no physician there?
Why then has the health of my poor people
  not been restored?" (Jer. 8:21–22)

At other times, images of healing are associated with the language
of rescue and relief:

The LORD, your God, is in your midst,
  a warrior who gives victory;
he will rejoice over you with gladness,
  he will renew you in his love;
he will exult over you with loud singing
  as on a day of festival.
I will remove disaster from you,
  so that you will not bear reproach for it.
I will deal with all your oppressors
  at that time.
And I will save the lame
  and gather the outcast,
  and I will change their shame into praise
  and renown in all the earth.
At that time I will bring you home,
  at the time when I gather you;
for I will make you renowned and praised
  among all the peoples of the earth,
when I restore your fortunes
  before your eyes, says the LORD. (Zeph. 3:17–20)

For Isaiah, salvation is peace with other peoples, harmony within the cosmos (for example, Isa. 2:1–5; 11:1–9).

This broader perspective on healing as one paradigm for grasping the meaning and experience of salvation may seem odd to those of us weaned on medical practices and health care systems in the modern Western world. It is often the case that we misconstrue the nature of healing in scripture by reading into the Bible alien notions of health and disease. We do this by focusing too narrowly the reach of "healing." In this respect it is worth remembering, first, that humanity was created in the image of God (Gen. 1:26–27); as we observed in the first chapter, this entails relationships of harmony within the human community as well as with God and the entire cosmos. Consequently, "healing" from a biblical perspective could never be limited to the physical body but must entail restoration to health in the fullest sense.

For example, when in Acts 3 Peter reports the healing of the lame beggar at the temple gate, he observes that "the faith that is through Jesus has given him this perfect health in the presence of all of you" (Acts 3:16). The term *holoklēria* refers to "wholistic health," and accounts for Luke's presentation of this man's healing as extending beyond his new ability to walk in order to embrace also his social and spiritual well-being. Note that, once he is raised up, the former lame beggar is able to enter God's house, the temple, with joy. We may hear in this account an echo of Isaiah 1:6, thus documenting that this former religiously blemished fellow is now without blemish, acceptable to the Lord, restored to God's people.

Second, we must remember that different cultures think of health, sickness, and healing in different ways, and this is true when one moves from the biomedical culture of the turn of the twenty-first century in the United States to the world of ancient Israel. Accordingly, for most of us, reading the biblical accounts of healing must be understood as an exercise in cross-cultural communication.

If "sickness" is any unwanted condition of self or substantial threat of unwanted conditions of self,[4] then notions of health and sickness are not "givens," as though all people at all times and in all places might represent themselves in the same way. Rather, ideas and

---

[4]I have adapted this definition from Robert A. Hahn, *Sickness and Healing: An Anthropological Perspective* (New Haven, Conn.: Yale Univ. Press, 1995), 22.

experiences related to "health" and "sickness" are immediately tied to how a people measure human well-being. It follows from this that accounts of sickness and hopes for health might take on different forms, as one moves from culture to culture. One system for classifying these accounts among medical anthropologists distinguishes between diseases, illnesses, and disorders:

- *Disease accounts* identify disease as an abnormality located within the body, at or beneath the skin. The problem lies in the structure and functions of bodily organs or systems. In this case, healing requires physical or biomedical intervention.
- *Illness accounts* take into account both the body but also one's networks of relationships and interaction with the larger social environment. The body is not discounted, but placed within a larger web of meaning where the focus is expanded beyond a biomedical concern with body parts and bodily systems to include the embodied lives of persons in community. Within this paradigm, "healing" might require physical intervention, but certainly must address the relationships of persons with others as part of the intervention.
- *Disorder accounts*, without neglecting the body and one's networks of relationships and interaction with a larger social environment, attend also to one's relationship to the world at large—unbalanced, out of order. The recovery of well-being, in this case, would be tantamount to "putting the world back together," or otherwise redressing a cosmic imbalance.[5]

Of course, as medical anthropologists are quick to point out, this taxonomy represents ideal categories that, in the lived experience of a people, may overlap. Nevertheless, it provides a helpful grid for making sense of the representation of salvation as healing in the world of the Bible.

We should observe, first, that modern westerners tend to think in terms of disease accounts. As a result, we tend to think of diseased individuals (rather than communities), what we label as "ailments"

---

[5]See Hahn, *Sickness and Healing*, 28; more generally, Bryon J. Good, *Medicine, Rationality, and Experience: An Anthropological Perspective*, Lewis Henry Morgan Lectures 1990 (Cambridge: Cambridge Univ. Press, 1994).

generally fall in the category of the physical or bodily, and cures are to be found in biomedical intervention. Happily, in recent decades, more constructive attention has been given to mental illness, but for the population as a whole the psychological constitutes a sphere of life separate from the physical. Only with slight hyperbole can Trinh Xuan Thuan remark, "To this day, the brain and mind are regarded as two distinct entities in Western medicine. When we have a headache, we consult a neurologist; when we are depressed, we are told to see a psychiatrist."[6] Given this understanding of things, it is no surprise that we tend to segregate healing (biomedical) from salvation (spiritual).

More pressing is how this understanding of reality, this life-world, artificially truncates our experience of well-being. Deeply committed to a biomedical model of health and healing, we focus our concerns and hopes on the life of one individual at a time. In such a world, the maintenance of human life and the reduction of physical suffering, at any cost, become the overriding concern. Physical health—with its often contrived notions of what is or ought to be "normal," and what is or ought to be "good-looking"—supplants any full-bodied (that is, *fully embodied*) sense of salvation.

People in the world of the Bible, and certainly within the biblical accounts, tended to think of sickness in more wholistic ways. For them, the source of sickness rested not only in the bodies of the sick, but also and sometimes especially in their social environments and in the larger universe. In this case, healing might entail restoring a person to community, some form of bodily intervention, the redress of cosmic imbalances—or, more typically, some combination of all of these.

A cross-cultural perspective on sickness and healing is important in making sense of many healing accounts in the Old and New Testaments, as well as when thinking about the relation of healing to salvation more generally. For example, in the Bible "leprosy" is rarely if ever true leprosy, or "Hansen's Disease." Rather, "leprosy" refers to any of a number of skin conditions that, when diagnosed by a priest, might render a person "unclean." According to Leviticus 13—14, leprosy is a sign of God's curse on a person; hence, someone diagnosed as a leper is marked as contagious and so forced to the margins of

---

Trinh Xuan Thuan, *Chaos and Harmony: Perspectives on Scientific Revolutions of the Twentieth Century* (Oxford: Oxford Univ. Press, 2001), 294.

human community. In and of itself, this sort of "leprosy" is not life-threatening, nor is it infectious in a biomedical sense, as though one might "catch" a skin disease from a "leper." In fact, when restored to health these lepers are not said to be "healed" but, rather, are "made clean." What we find here, then, is a valuable example of how religious, social, and physical maladies coalesce in a single set of symptoms within the world of the Bible. In the gospels, Jesus' intervention in such cases is classified as "cleansing" because religious impurity (and not a biological disease) has become the primary presenting problem. Intervention is followed by such instructions from Jesus as those found in Luke 5:14: "Go...and show yourself to the priest, and, as Moses commanded, make an offering for your cleansing, for a testimony to them." In these instances, the priest functions not as a healer but as a health care consultant, mediating the (former) leper's return to community with God's people.

In the same way, accounts of exorcism correlate spiritual, social, mental, and physical factors, both in the presentation of the disorder and in its resolution. The Gerasene demoniac lived not in a house but among the tombs (as though he were in quarantine, ritually unclean, isolated from human community, or as though he were dead), was naked and uncontrollable (and thus lacking personal identity and status as a human being), and his speech moves back and forth between "I"- and "we"-statements (crisis of personal identity). Following exorcism, he is sitting at the feet of Jesus (submission), clothed and in his right mind (returned to status as a human, with personal identity intact), and Jesus returns him to his home to declare what God had done for him (restored to his community, with a vocation) (Lk. 8:26–39).

In more straightforward accounts, too, such as the healing of the woman with a hemorrhage (Mk. 5:25–34), what might first be categorized as physical recovery (biomedical) is transparently bundled together with social and spiritual restoration. This is also true for the larger view of life wherein healing and sickness are indicators of Yahweh's favor and displeasure. Although one could never argue that health is necessarily the direct result of God's favor, nor that sickness is necessarily the direct result of divine punishment, it is nevertheless true that for ancient Israel there is a causal link from sin to sickness. (For examples, see Deut. 28; 1 Kings 13:1–25; Prov. 3:28–35; 11:19; 13:13–23; 1 Cor. 11:29–30. This theological position is eloquently represented by Job's interlocutors in Job 8:1–22; 11:6; 22:1–30, in a book where such logic is undermined!) In John 9, the disciples assume the causal relation of sin to physical disorder, but Jesus makes no general pronouncement on the subject; elsewhere, his actions presuppose the comparability of healing a man's paralysis and forgiving his sin (Mk. 2:1–12).

One more illustration: In Matthew 8—9, miraculous events seem to be lined up, one after the other, as the evangelist shows how Jesus makes available the presence and power of God's dominion to those dwelling on the margins of Jewish society in Galilee. Included are accounts that focus on a leper, the slave of a Gentile army officer, an old woman, the demonized, a paralytic, a collector of tolls, a young girl, and the blind. At the same time that Matthew recounts the restoration to physical health of those who are diseased, he also chronicles the restoration of persons to status within their families and communities, the faith-full reordering of life around God, and the driving back of demonic forces. Notice how the spectrum of images of healing converge in Matthew's recounting:

- Cleansing a leper allows him new access to God and to the community of God's people (Mt. 8:1–4).
- Healing a paralytic is comparable to forgiving his sins (Mt. 9:2–8).
- Extending the grace of God to toll collectors and sinners illustrates the work of a physician (Mt. 9:9–13).
- As throughout the biblical tradition, recovery of sight serves as a metaphor for the exercise of the insight of faith (Mt. 9:27–31).

Accordingly, with regard to healing, we should refuse attempts to divorce physical from spiritual or psychological ailment, or communal from physical disorder. A more wholistic approach to healing is demanded by the evidence. This is why "healing" serves so well as a way of articulating the biblical message of salvation.

Yahweh, the Healer

Throughout the scriptures of Israel, Yahweh's identity as healer is paramount: "I am the LORD who heals you" (Ex. 15:26). The context of Yahweh's self-description at this early juncture in Israel's life is crucial, for it follows the narration of the incredible lengths to which Yahweh has gone to liberate Israel from Egypt. "I am your healer," Yahweh declares, drawing attention to the powerful intervention of God on behalf of Israel, a power that is celebrated in the Song of Miriam: "Sing to the LORD, for he has triumphed gloriously; horse and rider he has thrown into the sea" (Ex. 15:21); and is on display in God's provision of sweet water in the desert (Ex. 15:25). Poetic language celebrates Yahweh's royal authority over Israel's enemies and the natural world, and acclaims the gift of salvation—and all of this is epitomized in the metaphor of healing.

In this same setting, Yahweh sets before the people an agreement: "If you will listen carefully to the voice of the LORD your God, and do what is right in his sight, and give heed to his commandments and keep all his statutes, I will not bring upon you any of the diseases that I brought upon the Egyptians; for I am the LORD who heals you" (Ex. 15:26). The remedy provided Israel generates a covenantal relationship: Israel must hearken to God's voice and heed God's commands; for God's part, rather than afflict the people with disease, as with Egypt, God will lavish them with health.

The Psalms similarly deploy the language of healing metaphorically to speak of God's blessings:

Bless the LORD, O my soul,
    and do not forget all his benefits—
who forgives all your iniquity,
    who heals all your diseases,
who redeems your life from the Pit,
    who crowns you with steadfast love and mercy,
who satisfies you with good as long as you live
    so that your youth is renewed like the eagle's.
The LORD works vindication
and justice for all who are oppressed. (Ps. 103:2–6)

Praise the LORD!
How good it is to sing praises to our God;
    for he is gracious, and a song of praise is fitting.
The LORD builds up Jerusalem;
    he gathers the outcasts of Israel.
He heals the brokenhearted,
    and binds up their wounds.
He determines the number of the stars;
    he gives to all of them their names.

> Great is our LORD, and abundant in power;
> his understanding is beyond measure. (Ps 147:1–5)

For our purposes, of special importance in these texts is the constellation of images within which Yahweh's work of healing is found. The concept of "healing" as divine gift rubs shoulders with Yahweh's care for and sovereignty over the cosmos, work of justice on behalf of the oppressed, extension of love and mercy, renewal of the fatigued, forgiveness, and restoration. Healing is God's setting things right.

Again in the Torah, as proof of Yahweh's singular status, Yahweh declares, "I kill and I make alive; I wound and I heal" (Deut. 32:39). Here is generous testimony to God's fidelity:

> Indeed the LORD will vindicate his people,
> have compassion on his servants,
> when he sees that their power is gone,
> neither bond nor free remaining.
> Then he will say: Where are their gods,
> the rock in which they took refuge,
> who ate the fat of their sacrifices,
> and drank the wine of their libations?
> Let them rise up and help you,
> let them be your protection!
> See now that I, even I, am he;
> there is no god besides me. (Deut. 32:36–39a)

This is the blessing reserved for those who acknowledge that God alone is God, who devote themselves wholly to God. This motif surfaces in a similar way in the latter portions of the Old Testament, as in 2 Chr. 7:11–14: If God's people will turn to God in prayer and humility, God will bring forgiveness and healing to their land. Yahweh binds up and heals the wounded (Job 5:17–18).

God's role as healer is even more pervasive among the prophetic writings, where appeals are made to God to come and heal both persons and the nation. Hezekiah appeals to God to restore his health (Isa. 38:16), and Ezekiel portrays Yahweh as healer of the weak, the sick, and the lost (Ezek. 34:16). The servant of Yahweh, Isaiah writes, will effect the healing of the people of God (Isa. 53:5). The prophet anticipates "the day when the LORD binds up the injuries of his people, and heals the wounds inflicted by his blow" (Isa. 30:26). The day is coming, the prophet announces, when God "will come and save you" (Isa. 35:4). The restoration of God's people is vividly linked to images signifying the restoration of health: "Then the eyes of the blind shall be opened, and the ears of the deaf unstopped; then the lame shall leap like a deer, and the tongue of the speechless sing for joy" (Isa. 35:5–6). It is not coincidence that we find in the gospels and Acts these acts of healing—indeed, this very vocabulary of restored health and celebration—signifying the advent of the anticipated era of salvation. (See below.)

Continuing our sketch of the biblical portrait of Yahweh as healer, in the New Testament healing is a sign of the in-breaking kingdom of God. This reminds us that, behind the healing ministry of both Jesus and his followers, stands Yahweh the healer. In Acts we learn that God worked deeds of power, wonders, and signs through Jesus so as to affirm the status of Jesus as God's authorized agent of salvation (Acts 2:22). In the same way, the Lord authorized the word of God's grace by "granting signs and wonders to be done" through Paul and Barnabas (Acts 14:3). Others may participate in God's healing activity, then, but this does not detract from the more fundamental affirmation that Yahweh is the one doing the healing. Indeed, the phrase so popular in Acts, "signs and wonders," is borrowed from Israel's scriptures, especially in reference to divine deliverance from Egypt. There, as in Acts, it broadcasts the actualization of God's saving purpose on behalf of God's people and testifies to God's healing influence in history.[7]

Jesus, Agent of God's Power to Heal

The portrait of Jesus as healer is central to the synoptic gospels: Matthew, Mark, and Luke. When we take into account that they sometimes contain multiple versions of the same episode, the list of independent accounts comprises six episodes of exorcism and seventeen accounts of healing (including three accounts of resuscitation). Jesus' ministry is distinguished by his *typical* behavior as a healer and his portrayal as one who exercised *in a direct way* the saving power of

---

[7]See, for example, Ex. 7:3; Deut. 4:34; 7:19; 26:8; 29:3; 34:11; Jer. 32:20–21; Dan. 4:2–3; 6:27; Acts 2:19, 22, 43; 4:30; 5:12; 6:8; 7:36; 8:6, 13; 14:3; 15:12.

God. He did not ask God to intervene on behalf of those in need of a miracle but pronounced their healing directly, in speech-acts that assumed his possession of divine authority to do so. He also often emphasized the component of faith in his ministry of healing—so much so, in fact, that one of the characteristic assertions of Jesus was, "Your faith has made you well."

Jesus often healed merely by pronouncement, but the gospel writers also mention his laying on of hands or touching the sick in the context of his healing. This was a boundary-crossing gesture of compassion that reflects the extension of God's own hand to act in creation and deliverance. This signifies the power of God at work in and through Jesus. That this practice is continued by Jesus' emissaries in Acts identifies them also as instruments of divine power.

According to the synoptic gospels, some who recognized Jesus' status as a healer did not see in his work divine credentials. Instead, they attributed his ministry of exorcism to his association with Satan. In dialogue with those persons, Jesus interprets his exorcisms as a sign of the work of the Spirit in his mission, and as a demonstration of God's kingdom at work among them (Mt. 12:24–33; Mk. 2:22–30; Lk. 11:14–26). Here, as elsewhere, the healing ministry of Jesus is portrayed as a sign of the in-breaking kingdom of God, as the divine blessings of salvation come near in the ministry of Jesus.

Accordingly, Jesus' healing ministry marked the coming of the new aeon, the long-awaited era of salvation. As we noted earlier, Isaiah 35:1–7 promises the coming of God in history to bring salvation and judgment, promising, among other things, "the eyes of the blind shall be opened, and the ears of the deaf unstopped." Similarly, in its Greek version, Isaiah 61:1–2 anticipates the coming of the end as a time when the blind would receive their sight. The relevance of this repeated Isaianic vision rests in the implicit and explicit use of that vision by the evangelists to indicate the significance of Jesus' ministry as a healer. Mark 7:37, for example, records how the crowds were astonished by a miracle of healing, and responded in words echoing Isaiah 35:5–6: "he even makes the deaf to hear and the mute to speak." Matthew 11:2–5 and Luke 7:18–22 (see Luke 4:18–19) recall in an explicit way the language and eschatological vision of Isaiah, and in doing so serve to communicate (1) that Jesus is God's anointed one and (2) that with Jesus' advent the new creation that fulfills the prophecies of Isaiah is unfolding. Jesus' perspective in Luke 11:20, though not tied into Isaianic expectations, is nevertheless comparable: "If it is by the finger of God that I cast out the demons, then the kingdom of God has come to you."

The healing activity of Jesus thus pointed beyond itself to the transformed nature of the times, to the new era being introduced in Jesus' coming. God's redemptive purpose was breaking into the world; the kingdom of God was already making its presence felt. Some of us today might be apt to see the significance of Jesus' healing ministry primarily in its miraculous character and wonder at these manifestations of supernatural power. In the gospels, though, their real importance lies elsewhere, in their witness to the reality that, in the presence of Jesus, the era of salvation had arrived, enabling people to live life again as God intended.

Jesus' healing was pivotal to the meaning of his ministry, declaring his identity as the authorized agent of Yahweh's healing beneficence, the presence of which signals in Jesus' ministry the currency of God's end-time rule. It is worth remembering, though, that this presentation of the nature of Jesus' ministry has not always been welcome. Those trying to make a name for themselves in the world and to fit into its designs are not likely to nurture hope for a messianic kingdom that will transform and renew everything. "Healing" is welcome only when "illness" is recognized. Only those who experience the pain of brokenness are likely to be hungry for "restoration." Civil religion, whether in the time of the Roman Empire or more modern days, is more likely to quash announcements of God's end-time rule than to support them. Religious institutions typically find themselves doing the same, in order to recommend themselves as representing fully God's interests on earth. Thus, for the Jewish leaders in Jerusalem, Jesus' healing activity marks him as a false prophet who manipulates God's people and subverts God's way, and is thus deserving of death (Lk. 23:1–5).

In Jesus' execution, marked as a false prophet accused of steering the people away from God through miracles of healing, we find a shocking reminder that not all welcome salvation with open arms. Some actually work against it, or deny it altogether.

The People of God as Community of Healing

From the perspective of scripture, the portrait of Yahweh as original giver and ongoing restorer of human life is both central and pervasive. This is true with respect to individuals (whose recovery, however, must be set within the network of their relationships with others and with

God) but also of the people of God, who depend upon God for life and renewal of life. Into this biblical story Jesus is introduced as the authorized agent of Yahweh's healing beneficence, the presence of which signals in Jesus' ministry the advent of God's end-time rule. As exalted Lord, Jesus is co-regent with God and dispenses the divine blessings of salvation, including both restored health (for which prayers are to be offered on behalf of the sick) and the Holy Spirit who enables gifts of healing.

What of other, human agents of healing? Priests, as we have noted, were not healers but rather health care consultants who might be called upon to verify a healing or cleansing. Prophets, on the other hand, were sometimes portrayed as agents of healing. Elijah was instrumental in restoring a widow's son to life (1 Kings 17:8–24), for example, and Elisha instructed Naaman, commander of the Syrian army, how to be cured of leprosy (2 Kings 5:1–15). According to Luke 4, Jesus mentions both of these episodes by way of articulating the nature of his own mission. In the New Testament, during the course of Jesus' ministry, his disciples participate in his ministries of healing and exorcism (for example, Mk. 6:7–13), and in Acts the ministries of the apostles, as well as of Stephen, Paul, and Barnabas, are characterized by signs and wonders, including healing. Such healing is performed explicitly in the name of Jesus (for example, Acts 3:1–10; 9:34; 16:16–18). This is evidence in support of the affirmation that, vindicated as Lord through his exaltation to the right hand of God, Jesus is now the one through whom the benefits of salvation are available. (See Acts 2:33–36.) Both Peter and Paul actually repudiate any notion that they have power to heal apart from Jesus (Acts 3:12–16; 14:14–15). For Luke, the healing activity of persons such as Stephen or Peter functions not only to convey the blessings of salvation now available through the risen Lord, but also to prove that people such as Stephen and Peter are the Lord's authorized emissaries.

In 1 Corinthians 12, Paul lists the gifts of healings and working of miracles as manifestations of the work of the Spirit in the life of the church. The use of the plural, "gifts of healings," suggests that each occasion of healing is a manifestation of this gift, as opposed to an individual claiming to possess permanently the power to heal. In 2 Corinthians, Paul speaks of his having performed the signs of an apostle (12:12; compare Rom. 15:18–19; 1 Thess. 1:5), which presumably would have included healing, but it is otherwise worth reflecting on how reticent Paul is to speak of such matters autobiographically. His own weakness is an occasion for identifying with the suffering of Jesus and for communicating the power of the gospel (for example, Gal. 4:13; 2 Cor. 12:7).

James directs those who are sick to call for the elders of the church to prayer over them, anointing them with oil in the name of the Lord (Jas. 5:14–16). James does not assume that illness is necessarily caused by sin, but does allow that sin may be a factor. In any case, sin must be confessed and it will be forgiven, with the result that the healing James envisages is multifaceted.

This cursory sketch gathers some of the more explicit evidence to indicate the role of God's people, both individually and collectively, in the healing work of God. Easily overlooked in such a survey is the importance of the witness to wholeness and integrity, including the health of the community, implied in such texts. Let us return to the letter of James, for example, where "salvation" is portrayed as restoring health in its expansive fullness.

> Are any among you suffering? They should pray. Are any cheerful? They should sing songs of praise. Are any among you sick? They should call for the elders of the church and have them pray over them, anointing them with oil in the name of the Lord. The prayer of faith will save the sick, and the Lord will raise them up; and anyone who has committed sins will be forgiven. Therefore confess your sins to one another, and pray for one another, so that you may be healed. The prayer of the righteous is powerful and effective. (Jas. 5:13–16)

Restoration of health is concerned with physical wellness, to be sure (Jas. 5:15), but not in a way that can be segregated from life more fully (Jas. 1:21; 5:20). Indeed, the interweaving of healing and forgiveness (Jas. 5:16) speaks to a vision of personhood that is wholly integrated. Likewise, life before God is worked out within a web of relationships within the Christian community, characterized by peace, care, and forgiveness (Jas. 2:13; 3:13, 17; 4:11–12; 5:16, 19).

Again, James does not equate sickness and sin, nor does he urge that sickness derives from sin. His perspective, rather, is that as sickness is to the human body so sin is to the church. Consequently, "healing" cannot be focused on a single person or on a single aspect of life. In fact, it is not too much to say that James presents ill health among individuals within the church as a test of the church. Our first instincts might be (and often are) to quarantine the sick. Typically, those who are not well—the weak, the hurting, the lonely, the diseased—become the targets of progressive isolation, usually through implicit acts or through simple neglect. If we do not isolate the sick by deliberately locating them in rooms to themselves, but rather by adopting behaviors that keep them at arm's length, does this make their segregation any less real? Will the community, and particularly its leadership, answer the summons of the sick, and gather around them with faith and prayer? Or will the sick find themselves progressively excluded from a community that is fearful of its own survival? Reflecting the character of God who is merciful and rich in compassion, the community of healing is one that is able to pray and confess sins together, confident in God's goodness.

Salvation as Healing: Expanding the Horizons

Thus far we have seen that "healing" has proven to be a remarkably rich metaphor for working out the nature of salvation in the biblical materials. Not only is it deployed in this way in both the Old and New Testaments, but when explored from the perspective of medical anthropology, the concept of healing has an impressive elasticity that promotes its usefulness for our purposes. The promise of "healing" presumes a shared definition of health and recognition of sickness, as well as the gracious presence of a healer. From scripture itself, we receive an all-encompassing perspective on human health in the cosmos and in relation to God, as well as well-developed ways of identifying the sickness that spreads like a cancer throughout the human family, even eating away at the world that humans call home. The term generally given this sickness in the Christian tradition is "sin," though, as we have seen in chapter 1, the term itself too easily limits conversation and masks the multivalent ways in which humans— individually, collectively, and systemically—neglect, deny, refuse to embody God's creative purpose. In this view, healing does not allow the categorization of the person or his or her salvation into "parts," as though inner and outer life could be separated. What is more, in a significant sense, healing does not allow us to think of the restoration of individuals, as it were, one at a time, but pushes our categories always to embrace the human community and, indeed, the cosmos.

Persons are not saved in isolation from the world around them. For healing, attention falls above all on the power and initiative of Yahweh as healer, and on Jesus, Yahweh's co-regent, through whom the renewing beneficence of God is made available. Finally, the metaphor of healing serves as an invitation to the people of God, not only to be recipients of God's good gifts of salvation, but also to be agents of healing, to be a community of compassion and restoration.

Scripture develops the metaphor of healing in its struggle to spell out the nature of God's salvation, but employs other concepts as well. In part, this is because all metaphors reveal some aspects of the reality to which they point while concealing others. More words are needed if we are to grasp as fully as possible the richness of God's beneficence. In part, this is because different people in different times and places need to have the nature of salvation spelled out in different terms— in terms, that is, which speak clearly and pointedly to their realities. The message of salvation requires a context for its articulation, and different contexts invite different articulations. It remains in this chapter, then, to comment briefly on several additional biblical motifs related to the theme of salvation, and especially on some that share kinship with the concept of healing.

Reconciliation is not known for its prominence as a term in the Bible. Related words appear only twenty-five times in the Old and New Testaments, but this should not keep us from noting, first, the important contexts in which these words appear (for example, Rom. 5:1–10; 2 Cor. 5:18–21; Col. 1:15–20) and second, how often the concept is present even when the term is missing. If Genesis 3 ends with God and the first humans on less-than-friendly terms, with humanity having actually recoiled in shame from God's presence, then it makes sense for much of scripture to locate its narratives and theology within the plotline of God's ongoing initiative to restore those relationships that had been broken. As Paul phrases it, "For if while we were enemies, we were reconciled to God through the death of his Son, much more surely, having been reconciled, will we be saved by his life" (Rom. 5:10); and, again: "In Christ God was reconciling the world to himself" (2 Cor. 5:19).

Reconciliation is a concept broad enough to embrace relationships between persons, and between humanity and God, as well as the relationship of humanity to the created order. The chronic division between Jew and Gentile is addressed in the cross of Christ, so that the dividing wall of separation has been razed (Eph. 2:11–22). The broken relationship between slave and master is not only bridged but, even more significantly, the newly restored relationship is to take on a different form, with slave and master comporting themselves as nothing less nor more than equals, "brothers" (Philemon). In the short letter of Philemon, then, Paul has undercut the moral basis of slavery, in the service of the gospel of reconciliation. Under the umbrella of reconciliation, even the cosmic forces, regarded as God's creation but now out of step with God's purposes, are restored to their purpose (Col. 1:15–20). The proclamation of reconciliation cannot be sundered from acts of reconciliation, and thus the message of salvation lays a claim on the everyday lives of people who are called to moral sensitivity and vigilance rooted in a life lived for others (2 Cor. 5:14—6:13).

Finally, it cannot be overemphasized that Paul does not develop the motif of reconciliation in mutual terms, as though the need for divine-human reparation were equal. "The world" may be estranged from God, and in need of restoration, but God is not estranged from the world. Thus, it is the world that stands in need of God's re-creative activity (hence, the language of "new creation" in 2 Cor. 5:17; Gal. 6:15).

The language of *new creation* is rare in the Old and New Testaments, but not the idea. One need only recall that classical formulation of hope in Isaiah, where the enmity between animals and humanity that resulted from the fall is overturned:

> The wolf shall live with the lamb,
>   the leopard shall lie down with the kid,
> the calf and the lion and the fatling together,
>   and a little child shall lead them.
> The cow and the bear shall graze,
>   their young shall lie down together;
>   and the lion shall eat straw like the ox.
> The nursing child shall play over the hole of the asp,
>   and the weaned child shall put its hand on the
>   adder's den.
> They will not hurt or destroy
>   on all my holy mountain;
> for the earth will be full of the knowledge of the LORD
>   as the waters cover the sea. (Isa. 11:6–9)

That this text is found in a larger passage related to the righteous rule of the messianic king (Isa. 11:1–5) plays an important role in Mark's gospel, where Mark comments on Jesus' temptation in the wilderness: "He was in the wilderness forty days, tempted by Satan; and he was with the wild beasts; and the angels waited on him" (Mark 1:13). The time is coming—indeed, it has already been introduced by Jesus—when the paradise of creation will be restored. Of course, this hope comes to its most profound expression in the image of "a new heaven and a new earth" in John's Revelation (Rev. 21:1). It is important to remember, though, that, in scripture, "new" often has the sense of "renewed," so that we should think in terms of both continuity and discontinuity: God's restoration will both embrace and transform the cosmos.

Wherever reconciliation is found, *forgiveness* is close by—not because reconciliation and forgiveness are synonymous, but because forgiveness is a precursor to reconciliation. That is, forgiveness is a necessary precondition to reconciliation. This distinction is crucial insofar as it underscores the nature of the problem and, thus, the character of the solution. Sin and its effects are taken with real seriousness in scripture. Forgiveness is extended not simply to persons, but to persons in light of their sins, their offenses. In order for full fellowship to be restored, sin and its effects must be taken seriously, forgiven, cancelled out. Although there may be forgiveness without reconciliation, there is no reconciliation without forgiveness.

Although there are examples of interpersonal forgiveness among men and women in the Old Testament (for example, Gen. 50:17; Ex. 10:17), by and large God is the one who forgives sin. In fact, forgiveness is within God's character: "To the Lord our God belong mercy and forgiveness, for we have rebelled against him" (Dan. 9:9). Says the Lord, "I, I am He who blots out your transgressions for my own sake, and I will not remember your sins" (Isa. 43:25). This is not to say that God is obligated to forgive, however, or that the granting of forgiveness is automatic, but rather flows out of the compassion and patience of Yahweh. "Who is a God like you, pardoning iniquity and passing over the transgression of the remnant of your possession? He does not retain his anger forever, because he delights in showing clemency" (Mic. 7:18).

Jeremiah anticipates the impending time when God would renew the covenant with the people, forgiving their iniquity and remembering their sin no more (Jer. 31:34). The advent of this era is announced in the Last Supper, as Jesus announces over the shared cup, "This is my blood of the covenant, which is poured out for many for the forgiveness of sins" (Mt. 26:28). In this context, we should remind ourselves that divine forgiveness was central to the recovery of Israel in the thought of Jews in the period of the Second Temple. To proclaim "forgiveness of sins" was to speak of God's acting to restore Israel as God's people.

In Luke and Acts, forgiveness is so important that it serves as a virtual stand-in for the language of salvation. Peter promises to those who repent, "Your sins will be wiped out" (Acts 3:19, author's translation). The blessings of salvation come into focus in the forgiveness that is available through Jesus (Acts 5:31; 13:43). It is important, therefore, that we grasp the obviously social dimension of forgiveness. Inasmuch as forgiveness was the means by which persons who had excluded themselves or had been excluded from the community of God's people might (re)gain entry into the community, the promise of forgiveness can never be reduced to talk about an individual's relationship to Yahweh. It is not surprising, therefore, that, in Jesus' teaching, divine forgiveness is correlated with the forgiveness we extend to one another (Lk. 11:4; Mt. 6:15). Jesus does not thereby establish a relationship of *quid pro quo* between divine and human forgiveness, as though God's extending forgiveness were dependent on human activity. Such a view would be flatly denied by Jesus' request that God forgive those responsible for his crucifixion (Lk. 23:34). Rather, Jesus grounds the disciples' request for divine forgiveness in their own practices of forgiveness. Jesus draws out the implications for human behavior from God's own activity. As he says elsewhere, "Be merciful, just as your Father is merciful" (Lk. 6:36). Hence, the embodiment of forgiveness in the practices of Jesus' disciples would be nothing less than an expression and imitation of God's own character.

If "reconciliation" is a concept borrowed from the world of interpersonal relations, *justification* finds its first home in the courtroom, so to speak (that is, at the city gates, where judgments were made and justice apportioned). This has led to a widespread misconstrual of "justification," as though it referred to salvation as little more than the abstract work of God in declaring someone "not guilty." In fact, in the world of Israel's scriptures, justification is a profoundly relational term, signifying faithfulness to the covenant.

"Justification" can be used with reference to God, then, on account of God's determined faithfulness to the covenant. In this case, the terminology of justification is typically translated in scripture with reference to the righteousness of God. Similarly, then, justification in relation to humanity would refer to the practice of unwavering faithfulness to the covenant into which God has entered with the human family. "Righteousness" is thus a guarantor of God's promises and a call upon humanity to keep covenant with Yahweh. "To be justified," in this reading, is to be included within covenant relationship with Yahweh. Paul employs a different idiom, but speaks to the same divine action, when he uses the language of *adoption* in Romans 8:15–23 and Galatians 4:5. Accordingly, God restores to a covenantal relationship those whose sin has led to their exile, and will even extend the lines of God's family to include all who believe; pouring upon them the spirit of adoption, God will make them God's own. Remembering that human identity and health are developed in essentially relational terms, we can easily grasp how the motif of justification and the related claim of divine adoption overlap with the notion of salvation-as-healing.

In the Old Testament, a penetrating example of justification is found in the person of Tamar, who plays the role of a prostitute, tricks Judah into fathering her sons, and yet is pronounced "more righteous" than he. This is because she has maintained the terms of the covenant while he has reneged on his covenant obligations (Gen. 38:1–26; see Deut. 25:5–10). A parallel idea is present in the Sermon on the Mount, wherein Jesus demands that the righteousness of his followers surpass that of the Pharisees and legal experts—that is, that their faithfulness to the covenant with Yahweh be more enduring (Mt. 5:20). In the letter of James, similarly, to be "justified" might more helpfully be translated, "to show to be righteous," since James's concern is that faith must express itself in faithfulness (Jas. 2:14–26). Paul's overall concern in his letter to the Romans is twofold, both having to do with justification: (1) Was God right to extend covenant relations to people who are outside of the law? (2) If not by means of Torah, how might persons be placed in covenant relation to God? The answer on both accounts is centered on the cross of Christ. God is shown to be "just" in the death of Jesus, just as sinners are brought into relationship with God through Jesus' death. How this is so is the concern of chapter 4.

Salvation as "healing" is also related to the biblical concept of *peace*, which moves far beyond the absence of war or conflict to denote the cosmos in a state of tranquility: the orderly creation in order, lacking nothing, dwelling in euphoria and harmony, all under the canopy of God's gracious rule. It is no wonder, then, that the Israelite greeting is a wish for peace, *Shalom!* Peace is of God (see Judg. 6:24; Rom. 16:20), and comes from God: "Peace, peace, to the far and the near, says the LORD; and I will heal them" (Isa. 57:19). In the latter parts of the Old Testament, peace is the focus of Israel's hope. Embracing the notions of security, justice, truth, and righteousness, peace is the divine blessing that will be poured upon God's people, with God's purpose restored and completed. Not surprisingly, then, the angels announce at Jesus' birth, "Glory to God in the highest heaven, and on earth peace among those whom he favors!" (Lk. 2:14), and salvation (in its most wholistic sense) can be pronounced in Jesus' words to those forgiven and healed, "Go in peace" (Mk. 5:34; Lk. 7:50). For Paul, as in Romans 5:1–2, peace refers to overcoming the breach separating God and humanity as well as the inauguration of new relations with God, together with the blessings that accompany life with God. Echoing Jesus' words of healing, Paul can write, "Let the peace of Christ rule in your hearts" (Col. 3:15). This text clearly points to the inner dimensions of the experience of peace, but this can be deceptive, as inner peace can never be segregated from peaceful relations with God, with the community of God's people, and from a commitment to and hope for God's gift of everlasting peace for all of creation.

The final motif we will introduce here has to do with salvation as *sanctification*, which refers to the holiness of the follower of Christ. In his discussion of the believer's comportment *vis-à-vis* the world at large, rather than condemning life in the world, Peter takes the positive route of characterizing his Christian audience in relation to God's call to holiness: "Instead, as he who called you is holy, be holy yourselves in all your conduct; for it is written, 'You shall be holy, for I am holy'" (1 Pet. 1:15–16). He thus locates the vocation of the saved squarely in the context of God's call upon Israel: "For I am the LORD who brought you up from the land of Egypt, to be your God; you shall be holy, for I am holy" (Lev. 11:45). As Leviticus 19 has it, family and community respect (vv. 3, 32), religious loyalty (vv. 3b, 4–8, 12, 26–31), economic relationships (vv. 9–10), workers' rights (v. 13), social compassion (v. 14), judicial integrity (v. 15), neighborly attitudes and conduct (vv. 11, 16–18), distinctiveness (v. 19), sexual integrity (vv. 20–22, 29), exclusion of the idolatrous and occult (vv. 4, 26–31), racial equality (vv. 33–34), and commercial honesty (vv. 35–36)—all of these commitments and practices are embraced in the call to holiness. In order for Israel to fulfil its mission of being Yahweh's priesthood in the midst of the nations (Ex. 19:6), God's people were to be "holy"—that is, "different," or "distinctive." This was not at root a call for segregation, but a model of engagement. To make a difference in the world of nations, Israel was to be different—in the words of Chris Wright, "recognizably, visibly, and substantively different, as the people belonging uniquely to Yahweh and therefore representing his character and ways."[8]

The Old Testament thus portrays holiness both as a reality of life (God calls out a people, making them distinctive) and a command (God calls that people to a particular way of life). God's people should be what they are, their doing should reflect their being; they are to live out their identity as God's people. For Paul, too, sanctification is a reality within which believers live and into which believers grow. This perspective is developed in part in Romans 6:19–23 (see also 1 Thess. 3—4), where we are told that it is impossible to be both a slave of sin and of righteousness. Rather, having been freed from sin and enslaved to God, believers are placed on the path that leads to sanctification. "Being holy," then, has an eschatological dimension (that is, it will be realized fully in the end time), but, on account of the grace of God, at work through the Holy Spirit, it is already a present experience and vocation of resisting evil and embracing moral purity. "Sanctification" reminds us that the salvation is ongoing, that "human health" is not a momentary affair but a gift and way of life.

Hebrews observes that Jesus was holy, blameless, pure (Heb. 7:26)—tempted, but without sin (Heb. 4:15). This perspective is worth looking at more closely. The perspective of Hebrews is that the Old Testament is incomplete in itself, and that the Old Testament actually points beyond itself, warning its readers not to make themselves too much at home there. One of its inadequacies is that

---

[8]Christopher J.H. Wright, "Old Testament Ethics: A Missiological Perspective," *Catalyst* 26 (2, 2000): 5–8 (6).

its prescribed means for dealing with sin, the priesthood and sacrifice, were incapable of leading persons on to the desired goal of perfection. This is overcome in Jesus in two ways. First, he is both the perfect priest and the perfect sacrifice, so that his self-offering can deal with human sinfulness once and for all. Second, and more to the point for our concerns here, he is the trailblazer or pioneer of human salvation, who opens up the path of perfect faithfulness. What sense does "perfect" have here? Clearly, moral goodness is related, but "perfection" cannot be limited to moral goodness in Hebrews. This is because Jesus, though "holy, blameless, undefiled, separated from sinners" (Heb. 7:26), had still to become perfect (Heb. 2:10; 5:7–9; 7:28). In this context, "perfect" has to do with Jesus' character, dispositions, and allegiances, *and* with his becoming fully qualified for the task before him. On the one hand, the writer emphasizes that Jesus, the pioneer of salvation, was like other humans in every respect, including the full experience of suffering and temptation, and yet walked faithfully the path of obedience to God. On the other, he thus presents Jesus as the one who opened up the road of holy living that others might follow—living by faith and prayer, entrusting himself to the God who is able to save him (5:7).

Epilogue

We have seen in this chapter what a marvelously elastic concept salvation is, in biblical perspective. This is not because "salvation" is hard to understand or difficult to tie down in a meaningful way. Rather, it is because salvation speaks to the wide diversity of our life experiences, all of them, all of us. It resists reductions of all sorts—to one "aspect" or "part" of the human person, or even to one person at a time. The terms we have explored, those related to healing and health, and more besides, shine an array of lights both on persons nested in all sorts of relations—with God, with the people of God, with the whole of the human community, and with God's good creation—and on the integrity and wholeness of individuals. Impulses and agents of healing bring all sin and all sin's effects into the realm of healing, brokenness of all kinds under the careful attentiveness and succor of the Healer.

Thinking of salvation in this way presses against our sensibilities, at least for many of us. We have grown accustomed to thinking of ourselves in isolated ways (my need, my treatment, my health) and in ways more segregated (spiritual versus physical, relational versus genetic). Nevertheless, it is precisely here that the witness of scripture holds out its promise and challenge. Rather than begging to be "applied" to our lives, seeking for its message to be molded to the contours of our worlds, the scriptures yearn to reshape and reconstitute the categories by which we comprehend our lives, our worlds, even our greatest needs. Reading scripture, we enter into its evaluation of our condition, but also encounter its promise of restoration, its hope of health.

The biblical theme of healing locates God at center stage. Before there can be talk of salvation, there is first talk of God. God-talk leads to salvation-talk. Theology pours forth as a curative, as a healing regimen, as soteriology. This is the God of the Old and New Testaments, whose work of restoration is displayed in Exodus, promised in the prophets, expressed definitively in Jesus, and even now is moving toward its completion in the end. New creation, forgiveness, reconciliation, peace, justification—these motifs and more are used in scripture to sketch the expansive grace of God at work in restoring us to health.

There is no escaping the human side of the equation, though, nor those forces that transcend the acts of human beings in their hapless pursuit of malady, disorder, and death. Those who know they are ill may desire a return to health, may welcome the gift of healing with arms open wide, but one of the tragedies of prolonged and pervasive illness is its ability to recreate itself as health, to mask infirmity as wellness, to blind us to the possibility of more and to our need for restoration. Having lost the capacity to feel, itself a symptom of our disease, we may not recognize our ill health, or perceive how close to the abyss of death is the pathway we traverse in our oblivion. Alternatively, our disease may cause us to turn on ourselves, and others, to pull away from or actively resist the gift and work of healing.

Those who are ill and seek wellness know that the return to health often involves struggle, and cost. Images of warfare come to mind: battling a virus, in the grip of a fever. Luke's gospel typically sees healing as a defeat of diabolic power, as release from malevolent shackles. And we have noted in the case of Jesus' own healing ministry that wellness-work is not always welcome. It is not enough to speak of Yahweh the healer, and salvation as healing, therefore. The biblical story is written with other chapters, illustrated with different images, especially those that congregate around the portrait of the divine warrior, Yahweh the liberator.

3

YAHWEH, THE LIBERATOR

"My soul magnifies the Lord,
    and my spirit rejoices in God my Savior,
for he has looked with favor on
        the lowliness of his servant.
    Surely, from now on all generations will call me blessed;
for the Mighty One has done great things for me,
    and holy is his name.
His mercy is for those who fear him
    from generation to generation.
He has shown strength with his arm;
    he has scattered the proud in the thoughts of their
        hearts.
He has brought down the powerful from their thrones,
    and lifted up the lowly;
he has filled the hungry with good things,
    and sent the rich away empty.
He has helped his servant Israel,
    in remembrance of his mercy,
according to the promise he made to our ancestors,
    to Abraham and to his descendants forever."
        (Luke 1:46–55)

These words comprise Mary's Song, the *Magnificat*, where God's mercy and covenant faithfulness are set side by side with Mary's portrait of God as the divine warrior whose incomparable power is on display in divine deliverance. God is the "Mighty One" who accomplishes "great things," who exhibits "strength" and scatters the proud, brings down the powerful from their thrones, and sends the rich away empty. This is the God who engages in battle on behalf of God's people, who performs dynamic acts.

It is important that we reflect seriously on these words from the gospel of Luke as we begin this examination of the biblical presentation of God the liberator who triumphs over those who oppose God. This is because Christians too often relegate the portrait of God the warrior to the Old Testament, sometimes even juxtaposing the God of the Old Testament with the God of the New, Warrior versus Friend, military might versus compassion and grace. But here, in a passage that epitomizes the nature of the good news in Luke's gospel, we find this presentation of Yahweh as the champion who saves Israel from those who would oppress them. Mary paints a portrait with hues resplendent already in the Old Testament, evoking long and deep reminiscences of God's mighty act of deliverance in the exodus from Egypt and of the divine promises in the prophets of the coming deliverance.[1]

It is true that the image of God at war is evident more generally in the Old Testament, and especially in Deuteronomy and the historical books. Old Testament scholar Tremper Longman III has identified a pattern woven into this theological tapestry. First, Yahweh reveals to Israel that war is pending, and thus when and whom they were to engage in battle. Israel is to enter war not on its own initiative, but according to God's behest. For example, Joshua 5:13–15 narrates a divine visitation in which the warrior God outlines for Joshua the strategy to defeat Jericho, whereas later, in Joshua 9, Joshua displeases God by his decision not to proceed with battle. The sacred character of warfare is signaled in these narratives by divine initiative, and also by the rituals that accompany preparation—the offering of sacrifices, for example (1 Sam. 13:1–15).

---

[1] Richard A. Horsley, *The Liberation of Christmas: The Infancy Narratives in Social Context* (New York: Crossroad, 1989), 111.

Second, pains are taken to ensure the presence of God in the midst of battle, signified by the presence of the ark of the covenant with Israel's armies. (See Num. 2.) If Yahweh is present, then Israel need not (and must not) depend on more potent weapons, more stalwart defenses, or superior numbers. Indeed, Gideon is informed that the combatants in his employ are too numerous: "The LORD said to Gideon, 'The troops with you are too many for me to give the Midianites into their hand. Israel would only take the credit away from me, saying, "My own hand has delivered me"'" (Judg. 7:2). The result is that the army must be reduced in numbers. Similarly, though Goliath had a bronze helmet, a coat of mail (that weighed 5,000 shekels of bronze!), greaves of bronze on his legs, a bronze javelin, a huge spear, and a shield-bearer to accompany him, David refused all armament, save the staff befitting a shepherd, five smooth stones, and a sling (1 Sam. 17). According to the psalmist, "A king is not saved by his great army; a warrior is not delivered by his great strength. The war horse is a vain hope for victory, and by its great might it cannot save" (Ps. 33:16–17). In the face of battle, says Israel, "Our pride is in the name of the LORD," not in chariots or horses (Ps. 20:7). Finally, after the battle has been engaged, praise is given to Yahweh. Israel, when obedient, wins the war because of the power of Yahweh.[2]

However, the prominence of warfare and of the portrait of God as liberator in the Old Testament should not mask the importance of these images in the New Testament. Jesus himself engages in warfare, for example, and in the book of Revelation John the Seer envisions a great and final battle leading to the defeat of God's enemies. If the nature of this warfare is nuanced in various ways, if the enemies wear different masks and the weapons used against them derive from a different armory, this does not detract from the centrality of the theme of Yahweh the liberator in biblical soteriology. The opponents of God and God's purpose and actions are many and powerful, and these cannot be placated or simply fooled but must be defeated if God's creation is to enjoy salvation in all of its fullness.

In this chapter, then, we turn our attention to images of Yahweh the liberator in scripture. Our focus will be on the definitive and

[2]Tremper Longman III and Daniel G. Reid, *God Is a Warrior,* Studies in Old Testament Biblical Theology (Grand Rapids, Mich.: Zondervan, 1995); Longman, "Warfare," in *New Dictionary of Biblical Theology,* ed. T. Desmond Alexander and Brian S. Rosner (Downers Grove, Ill.: InterVarsity, 2000), 835–39 (836–37).

paradigmatic act of liberation in scripture, the exodus from Egypt, together with the hopes for deliverance this event activated in Israel's imagination. This will take us to traditions related to the expectation of new exodus in the latter pages of the Old Testament, as well as the announcement of the actualization of God's promises in the advent of Jesus Christ. This discussion will raise several pressing questions: Given that the exodus from Egypt seems clearly focused on the liberation of a people, what of the liberation of the cosmos? What can "liberation" mean in the context of the Roman Empire? And, in what sense can we speak of God's people "at war"? Throughout this chapter we will see how such related motifs as redemption and ransom, deliverance and rescue, are woven together in scripture.

Exodus as a Paradigm of Israel's Salvation

The fresco of Israel's scriptures is splattered with images of exodus, with scores of unambiguous references to, and hundreds of echoes of, this foundational event in the life of God's people. References, whether explicit or implicit, to the exodus from Egypt are found in all of the Old Testament's subsections: law, historical narrative, writings, and prophets. Exodus is alive in the memory of God's people, not only as historic event but also as the lens through which to make sense of present experience and as the matrix within which to shape future hopes. Clearly, the identity of Israel as a people—indeed, as God's people—comes into focus in the exodus: in Israel's deliverance from Egypt, the journey through the wilderness and reception of the law at Sinai, and entry into the land of promise. It is not only God's people who gain an identity here, however. God first reveals God's own identity in this story: "I AM WHO I AM" (Ex. 3:14); and from Exodus onward, this God is known as "the LORD your God, who brought you out of the land of Egypt, out of the house of slavery" (Ex. 20:2).[3]

The story is anticipated already in Genesis, where God predicted to Abraham, "Know this for certain, that your offspring shall be aliens in a land that is not theirs, and shall be slaves there, and they shall be oppressed for four hundred years; but I will bring judgment on the nation that they serve, and afterward they shall come out with great possessions" (Gen. 15:13–14). However macabre this turn of events

---

[3]Compare, for example, Ex. 29:46; Lev. 11:45; 19:36; 22:33; 25:38; 26:13; Num. 15:41; 23:22; 24:8; Deut. 1:30; 5:6; 8:14; 13:5; et al.

might have seemed in prospect (in the case of Abraham) or in reality (in the case of Abraham's descendants), it is precisely through this means that God would accomplish those covenant promises to Abraham, to make of him a great and mighty nation, many in number occupying a vast expanse of land (Gen. 12:2, 7; 13:14–17; 15:5, 18; 18:18). As Joseph had observed to his brothers, whose malicious plans had led to his enslavement, "Even though you intended to do harm to me, God intended it for good, in order to preserve a numerous people, as he is doing today" (Gen. 50:20; see Gen. 37–50). Albeit in microcosm, in this way God would establish a new humanity, provide Israel with a land fit for the gods, and live among them: "I will take you as my people, and I will be your God" (Ex. 6:7). What is more, through this sequence of events, God demonstrates both the inclination to hear the distressed cries of the oppressed and the nature of God's intervention not only to alleviate that distress but to form among the marginal a people called to embody God's own character. (See Deut. 26:5–10.)[4]

The opening chapter of Exodus orients us to what is at stake. Interestingly, it is Pharaoh himself who first declares of this rag-tag confederation of clans that they are a "people," "numerous and… powerful" (Ex. 1:1–9). Pharaoh thus gives voice to God's own plan, even if his own intent and actions were set in defiance of God's words. Labeling the Hebrew people thus, Pharaoh pronounces an official ideology capable of justifying their enslavement—not first as a means of deploying them in his colossal building programs, as we might have anticipated, but, more importantly, as a means of social control: "'Come, let us deal shrewdly with them, or they will increase and, in the event of war, join our enemies and fight against us and escape from the land.' Therefore they set taskmasters over them to oppress them with forced labor" (Ex. 1:10–11). In a series of moves, Pharaoh first enslaves the Hebrews, then tries secretly to slaughter their sons, and finally decrees publicly, "Every boy that is born to the Hebrews you shall throw into the Nile, but you shall let every girl live" (Ex. 1:22). The circumstances sketched here are heinous by any human measure, and it is no wonder that the Israelites are said to groan and cry out (Ex. 2:23). For our purposes, it is crucial that we place the

---

[4]Norbert F. Lohfink, *Option for the Poor: The Basic Principle of Liberation Theology in the Light of the Bible* (Berkeley, Calif.: Bibal, 1987), 27–52.

perhaps more obvious suffering and oppression of Israel side by side with the concomitant reality that, in adopting his solution to the problem of the burgeoning of Abraham's descendants, Pharaoh has usurped the role of God and contravened God's promise of blessing. At the other end of the story, then, we recognize that God liberates Israel so as to transform their status from a people enslaved to Egypt to persons who may serve God alone: "So now, O Israel, what does the LORD your God require of you? Only to fear the LORD your God, to walk in all his ways, to love him, to serve the LORD your God with all your heart and with all your soul." (Deut. 10:12).[5] This transformation would entail the deconstruction of Egyptian idolatry, the humiliation of Egypt and its gods through the ten plagues visited upon Egypt through God's mighty hand and outstretched arm, as well as the destruction of Egypt's army: "horse and rider he has thrown into the sea" (Ex. 15:1).

Biblical theologian Walter Brueggemann has gathered together the series of verbs used in Israel's testimony to "Yahweh, the God Who Delivers."[6]

- Yahweh *brings out*—that is, the movement of Israel is geographical, from one location to another (e.g., Ex. 6:6; 13:3). This movement entails liberation, however, and not simply resettlement, since it is not at Israel's initiative. God is the agent who propels his people out of the land of oppression. We may add that this decisive act on God's part did not come by means of God's working within the borders of Egypt to cause a redistribution of goods and services, for example, but through the re-creative act of forming a people from among those who were not a people (Hos. 1:9; 2:23; 1 Pet. 2:10). In the most graphic terms, the Out-of-Egypt-Bringing God has established a Not-Like-Egypt People.
- Yahweh *delivers*—that is, God acts powerfully, forcefully, to rescue Israel from danger (e.g., Ex. 3:8; 14:30). This bespeaks the divine struggle with those powers that threaten the well-being of God's people, powers that Israel itself was impotent to counter.

---

[5] See Ex. 4:23; 7:16; 8:1; 9:1, 13; 10:3, 26; 14:12; Göran Larsson, *Bound for Freedom: The Book of Exodus in Jewish and Christian Traditions* (Peabody, Mass.: Hendrickson, 1999), 5–15.

[6] The outline of what follows is adapted from Walter Brueggemann, *Theology of the Old Testament: Testimony, Dispute, Advocacy* (Minneapolis: Fortress Press, 1997),173–76.

- Yahweh *redeems*—that is, God takes the role of kinsperson to the marginal, intervening on their behalf to forestall the downward spiral of violence against oppressed Israel (e.g., Ex. 6:6; 13:15; 15:13). This is not the redemption of slaves through purchase, as one might expect from the economic connotations of the term "redeem," but the emancipation of the enslaved and their restoration to wholeness in relation to God.

- Yahweh *brings up*—that is, when God leads Israel from one place to another, from the land of slavery to the land of promise, God also reverses their status (for example, Ex. 3:8, 17). Human refuse, dregs of the social order, these are the ones whom God raises up, exalting them. To look to a later event in Israel's history, if Daniel hardly seems to fit the description of "refuse" or "dregs," he is looked upon by the elite as a misfit and threat. And it is clear that his rescue by God from the den of lions constituted for him a reversal of status. The victim of political intrigue, thrown to the lions, but protected by God, he is "taken up out of the den" of lions, his God exalted, and he prospered while his enemies were destroyed (Dan. 6). As Mary will later celebrate, "He has brought down the powerful from their thrones, and lifted up the lowly" (Lk. 1:52).

In all these ways, and more, Israel testifies to the exodus as the act of God, and thus to the people's existence and character as a nation purposed and established by Yahweh the liberator. It is this act that is celebrated in the Song of Moses, and of Miriam:

"I will sing to the LORD, for he has triumphed
     gloriously;
  horse and rider he has thrown into the sea.
The LORD is my strength and my might,
     and he has become my salvation;
this is my God, and I will praise him,
     my father's God, and I will exalt him.
The LORD is a warrior;
     the LORD is his name.
Pharaoh's chariots and his army he cast into the sea;
     his picked officers were sunk in the Red Sea.
The floods covered them;
     they went down into the depths like a stone.

> Your right hand, O LORD, glorious in power—
>> your right hand, O LORD, shattered the enemy.
> In the greatness of your majesty you overthrew your
>> adversaries;
>> you sent out your fury, it consumed them like
>> stubble.
> At the blast of your nostrils the waters piled up,
>> the floods stood up in a heap;
>> the deeps congealed in the heart of the sea.
> The enemy said, "I will pursue, I will overtake,
>> I will divide the spoil, my desire shall have its fill of
>> them.
>> I will draw my sword, my hand shall destroy
>> them."
> You blew with your wind, the sea covered them;
>> they sank like lead in the mighty waters.
> Who is like you, O LORD, among the gods?
>> Who is like you, majestic in holiness,
>> awesome in splendor, doing wonders?
> You stretched out your right hand,
>> the earth swallowed them.
> In your steadfast love you led the people whom you
>> redeemed;
>> you guided them by your strength to your holy
>> abode...
> The LORD will reign forever and ever."
>> (Ex.15:1–13, 18)

This song is worth reflecting on at length, but here I will underscore only two major concerns. First, unlike songs of victory in the ancient world, this one is emphatic in its singular focus on the work of God. No king occupies central stage. Not even Moses, agent of deliverance, comes in for recognition. We find no hint of self-congratulation on the part of Israel. Salvation belongs to God.

Second, we should observe the degree to which exodus from Egypt has been cast in terms borrowed from the story of creation. In the images of divine action, the spreading of the waters, the divine breath, and more, the story of beginnings finds its reprise in intervention and exodus. "In a trembling moment, the world is brought back to the chaotic situation 'in the beginning,' when an act of divine creation is needed to overcome chaos."[7] Liberation appears as new creation.

New Exodus: Hope in Memory

It is difficult to overestimate the dynamic of the exodus story in Israel's ongoing life and identity. Recent work in neuroscience has brought to our attention how central meaning-making is to our day-to-day experience, and to what lengths we will go to construct stories that provide a context for understanding and interpreting our perceived realities. Apparently, one of the distinguishing characteristics of the human family, when compared with other inhabitants of the earth, is this capacity for and drive toward making sense, storied sense, of our experienced world.[8] A perusal of the scriptures of Israel with an ear tuned to the resonances of the exodus will indicate how this event has guided the meaning-making activity of Israel, how profoundly the exodus story was imprinted on the thought patterns of Israel's collective memory. Life rarely comes to us with built-in structures and meaning. By situating the story of our lives within a larger narrative, we find both structure and meaning, and this is precisely the creative effect of exodus, the story of which was to be told and retold in every household, year after year:

> A wandering Aramean was my ancestor; he went down into Egypt and lived there as an alien, few in number, and there he became a great nation, mighty and populous. When the Egyptians treated us harshly and afflicted us, by imposing hard labor on us, we cried to the LORD, the God of our ancestors; the LORD heard our voice and saw our affliction, our toil, and our oppression. The LORD brought us out of Egypt with a mighty hand and an outstretched arm, with a terrifying display of power, and with signs and wonders; and he brought us into this place and gave us this land, a land flowing with milk and honey. (Deut. 26:5–9)

Importantly, this was not an exercise in memorization and recitation, nor is the rehearsal of this story motivated by antiquarian

---

[7]Larsson, *Bound for Freedom*, 102.

[8]See James B. Ashbrook and Carol Rausch Albright, *The Humanizing Brain: Where Religion and Neuroscience Meet* (Cleveland: Pilgrim Press, 1997).

interests. Indeed, Passover did not happen to "people way back then." It happened to *us*, to *our people*. The story of the exodus *is* our story. Successive generations thus write themselves into this story of Israel's origins—when God created a "people," rescuing them from genocidal slavery and, taking their enemies as God's own, proved the unassailable and unrelenting opponent of human oppression—and give their life together meaning within its horizons.

In Israel's scriptures, this process of community formation around the exodus has had two significant effects. The first consequence is a people whose imagination is determined by the liberating initiative and leadership of God. The second consequence is the exodus-shaped hope that would emerge, guiding Israel into its future and playing so central a role in the pages of the New Testament. By "imagination," I refer to what theologians call "...the power of taking something as something by means of meaningful forms, which are rooted in our history and have the power to disclose truths about life in the world."[9] That is, I refer to "imagination" or "life-world" as the often invisible spectacles through which we perceive and construct a unified sense of ourselves, and our interactions with others, and, indeed, with the cosmos. Here are the categories by which we construe and experience life, conceive of its unity, and reckon its form and integration. Generally, this life-world is not systematically articulated, but is operative typically at the unacknowledged level of day-to-day life. To speak of the importance of the exodus in Israel's imagination, then, is to signal how Israel's experience of the God who liberated them from the iron grip of Pharaoh, and who led them through the wilderness to Sinai and on to "a land flowing with milk and honey," has provided the means by which Israel comprehends the world. Formed around this experience and image of God, Israel sees itself not as one nation among many, but as occupying a place of responsibility within the grand narrative of the outworking of God's purpose from creation to new creation.

As a result, the exodus story is not found in the mothballs of antiquity, but seems always on the tip of the tongue. Indeed, God's people understand that the activity of God, definitively expressed in Exodus, lies at the forefront of God's own declarative memory and is

---

[9]David J. Bryant, *Faith and the Play of Imagination: On the Role of Imagination in Religion,* Studies in American Biblical Hermeneutics 5 (Macon, Ga.: Mercer Univ. Press, 1989), 5.

a transparent window into God's own character. And why not? After all, the exodus is God's own signature, celebrated annually in the Festival of Passover. Exodus is the ground and warrant of Torah, and the giving of Torah at Sinai marks nothing less than the creation of a people whose corporate life was to reflect God's own character. The images are everywhere. The story of the exodus is fused with the story of the conquest of Canaan (Joshua), with Joshua portrayed as a new Moses. Indeed, Joshua 3—4 reports the rise of Joshua as Israel's leader, the crossing of the Jordan by Israel in a scene filled with reverberations of the Red Sea crossing, and the branding of Israel's deliverance on the landscape of Israel's collective memory. The building of the temple under Solomon is dated from the exodus (1 Kings 6:1), and the coming of the glory of God upon the temple at its dedication is presented as the culmination of the exodus (1 Kings 8). Moral decay in Israel under Solomon and Rehoboam is reminiscent of Egypt, and Jeroboam's return from Egypt to deliver his people echoes the story of Moses and Aaron (1 Kings 11—12). In the Psalms, hymns of praise celebrate the exodus (for example, Pss. 66, 68, 105), psalms of lament appeal to God's mighty act of deliverance (for example, Pss. 74, 77, 80), and numerous texts draw upon the memory of the exodus to contrast the powerful deeds and faithful mercy of God with the faithlessness of God's people. Amos, Hosea, and Micah, to mention only three of God's spokespersons, paint Israel's infidelity with patterns taken either from Egypt or from Israel's rebellion in the wilderness, while portraying Yahweh as the faithful, liberating God who would restore Israel. In these and countless other texts, the scriptures weave the story of Israel's life with strands of yarn spun out of Exodus.[10]

Efforts at casting the hope of Israel in the well-formed patterns of the exodus reach their zenith in Isaiah, and especially Isaiah 40—66. Israel is now in exile on account of its drawing back from its life as a people formed by the exodus, its having withdrawn from covenant partnership with God. What hope remains? Just as God had warred against Egypt so as to deliver Israel, so, when Israel patterned its life after oppressive Egypt, God had clashed with Israel. Even so, God's judgment against Israel would not be the final word. Importantly, the promise of restoration is formed in the mold of exodus. The book of Isaiah reaches a turning point with chapter 40, insisting that the age

<hr/>

[10]Cf. Rikki E. Watts, "Exodus," in *New Dictionary of Biblical Theology*, 478–87 (482–84).

of restoration remained a future hope but declaring the certainty of that hope nonetheless. In the exodus, God delivered the Hebrew people from Egyptian subjugation, forming them into God's own people, and leading them to the land of promise. In the new exodus, God would deliver the people from captivity and exile, restoring them as God's people. Apparently, the only way to characterize Israel's reformation and restoration as God's people is to evoke the story that belongs to the founding moment of Israel's life, the story of the exodus. This shows, however, that the story of the exodus was not the possession of Israel's past but was vibrant and potent in the people's ongoing life and self-understanding. At the center of this story was God: "The LORD is a warrior" (Ex. 15:3) — "The LORD goes forth like a soldier, like a warrior he stirs up his fury; he cries out, he shouts aloud, he shows himself mighty against his foes" (Isa. 42:13).

In the hands of Isaiah, the exodus story is transformed for its role in the service of new exodus hope.[11] First, the pattern of exodus has been reformulated as a future event predicated on the merciful, powerful act of God in Israel's past. Second, taking up threads already evidenced in the Song of Moses (Ex. 15), Isaiah recasts the exodus pattern in ways that meld the restoration of Israel with the restoration of the cosmos itself. New exodus thus merges into new creation. Third, the identity of God's people is expanded in a way that recalls the promise to Abraham, who was to be the father of many nations (Gen. 17:4–5) and not only of Israel. Says the Lord,

> It is too light a thing that you should be my servant to raise up the tribes of Jacob and to restore the survivors of Israel; I will give you as a light to the nations, that my salvation may reach to the end of the earth. (Isa. 49:6)

This demonstrates the importance of the story of the exodus for the past, present, and future work of sorting out the identity of God's people. Integral to this universalistic emphasis is a further concern of central importance—namely, the grounding of the claim that Yahweh alone is God and the concomitant rejection of idolatry in all of its forms. Indeed, the sovereign power of God is manifest in liberating,

---

[11]See especially David W. Pao, *Acts and the Isaianic New Exodus*, Wissenschaftliche Untersuchungen zum Neuen Testament (Tübingen, Germany: Mohr/Siebeck, 2000) 2:130.

restorative acts, a claim that could never be made on behalf of the idols of the nations. (See Isa. 40:12–31; 41:1–10; 44:9–20; 46:1–13.) Finally, the Isaianic vision of a new exodus identifies the performative word of God as the instrument by which God would deliver and restore the people. The mighty hand and outstretched arm of the Lord are eclipsed by the word as the means by which God's liberating purpose is actualized. God's word will stand forever (Isa. 40:9); "it shall not return to me empty, but it shall accomplish that which I purpose, and succeed in the thing for which I sent it" (Isa. 55:11). And here is that word, which, says the Lord, "has gone forth in righteousness," that "word that shall not return: 'To me every knee shall bow, every tongue shall swear'" (Isa. 45:23; cf. Phil. 2:6–11).

Each in its own way, the opening books of the New Testament pick up and continue the story of Israel, as do other New Testament witnesses. After providing for Jesus an ancestral record, for example, the narrative of the gospel of Matthew opens with an account of the birth of Jesus that is reminiscent of the story of Moses. At the forefront of this parallelism is the attempt of a malevolent ruler to murder the future liberator of God's people, a scheme that is frustrated even though it leads to the execution of other children. In both accounts, Egypt figures centrally, and a period of exile leads finally to the deliverer's return to his own people where he engages in a divine vocation of bringing salvation to Israel (Mt. 2).

Even more important than these hints of Jesus' status as the new Moses (cf. Deut. 18:15–18), however, is the evidence Matthew provides that Jesus embraces the role of true Israel, together with the many echoes to Israel's scriptures urging the view that, with Jesus' advent, the hoped-for new exodus has begun. For example, with regard to Jesus' exile in Egypt, Matthew declares that the child is thus replicating the historic journey of Israel. Citing Hosea 11:1, a text that speaks of Israel's escape from its oppressors in the ancient past, Matthew writes, "This was to fulfill what had been spoken by the Lord through the prophet, 'Out of Egypt I have called my son'" (Mt. 2:15). Again, after his baptism, Jesus' responses to the devil's wilderness temptations are each drawn from the experience of Israel en route from Egypt to the promised land. Whereas Israel's testing in the wilderness had led again and again to failure, however, Jesus proves himself to be faithful—indeed, to be the authentic son of God, true

Israel (Mt. 4:1–10; Deut. 8:3; 6:16, 13). The message of the kingdom of God is articulated by John the Baptist in relation to Isaiah's prophecy of a new exodus (Mt. 3:1–3; Isa. 40:3), and liberation is secured by the Isaianic servant (Mt. 20:28; Isa. 53:6–12). Some interpreters have seen in the presence of five major discourses of Jesus in the gospel of Matthew evidence that Matthew portrays Jesus as the new Moses presenting a new Torah. The relation of Jesus' ministry of healing to his role as the Isaianic servant in concert with Isaiah's new exodus is also made explicit in the narrative (Mt. 8:17; 11:5; Isa. 35:5–6; 53:4; 61:1–2).

Within Matthew's gospel, this emphasis on the new exodus is not first and foremost a matter of christological interest, as though the evangelist's primary purpose had to do simply with identifying the nature of Jesus for his audience. Rather, Matthew's agenda is pointedly ecclesiological, concerned with the nature of the church and its relation to the purpose and activity of God among the people of Israel. Just as the events surrounding the exodus were concerned with the calling out and formation of a people through liberation, so Jesus had come to "save his people from their sins" (Mt. 1:21) *and*, in doing so, to form a people, comprising the church, who gather in allegiance and submission and who carry out the mission that takes its direction and authority from Jesus himself (Mt. 28:18–20). As God had promised to Abraham, and as anticipated in images of the new exodus found in Isaiah, according to Matthew, God's renewed people would include "many nations" (cf. Mt. 8:5–13; 21:43). And just as God had been present to Israel—in the pillar of fire and cloud— on the exodus journey, so is God "with us" in the advent and ongoing presence of Jesus (Mt. 1:23; 28:20).

Similar threads are woven into the cloth of 1 Peter, an epistle in which the historical distinction between Israel of old and the author's own audience is collapsed in the service of theological identity. Images of exodus and exile, both drawn from Israel's past, form the texture of Peter's portrayal of his audience: They are people on a journey, sojourners, aliens—metaphors that speak to the oppression experienced (yet again) by God's people, the temporary nature of the experience of diaspora in which the people of God are depicted as a journeying people (for example, 1 Pet. 1:3–12), and the possibility and threat of assimilation and defection. In a wonderful patchwork of images borrowed from Israel's journey, Peter emphasizes the character and hope of his audience as God's people: "But you are a chosen race, a royal priesthood, a holy nation, God's own people, in order that you may proclaim the mighty acts of him who called you out of darkness into his marvelous light. Once you were not a people, but now you are God's people; once you had not received mercy, but now you have received mercy" (1 Pet. 2:9–10). Here are strong reverberations from Ex. 19:1–6 and Isa. 43:20–21, exodus account and new exodus promise, through which Israel has gained its particular self-awareness, centered in its status as a community liberated, gathered, and led by Yahweh. The honorable status of God's people addressed by Peter could hardly be more profoundly highlighted. At the same time, the membership of these people within the community of God's people could hardly stand in more stark contrast to their marginal status within the world at large, where they did not belong, had no real home, and suffered the indignities of alienation, dislocation, and venomous ostracism. Abhorred among the nations, these Gentiles now share in the elect and precious status of God's covenantal people. As Isaiah had written of the coming new exodus, "Thus says the LORD, the Redeemer of Israel and his Holy One, to one deeply despised, abhorred by the nations, the slave of rulers, 'Kings shall see and stand up, princes, and they shall prostrate themselves, because of the LORD, who is faithful, the Holy One of Israel, who has chosen you'" (Isa. 49:7).

Matthew's gospel and 1 Peter are only two of many New Testament witnesses to the pervasiveness of the theme of new exodus in early Christianity. The identification of Jesus as "our Passover lamb" (1 Cor. 5:7, author's translation), images of the journeying people of exodus as a model for the Corinthian community (1 Cor. 10:1–4), the roots of the language of "redemption" (for example, Lk. 2:38; Rom. 3:24) deep in the soil of exodus-reflection (for example, Deut. 7:8; 9:26; Pss. 25:22; 26:11) and promise of new exodus (for example, Isa. 41:14; 43:1)—these and myriad other texts point to the ongoing significance for biblical theology of understanding salvation in terms of exodus and of the biblical portrayal of Yahweh as liberator.

The Depth and Breadth of Liberation

Given the pervasiveness of the theme of liberation, two questions might be raised. First, how does the work of God to deliver the oppressed figure into God's concern for the welfare of the whole of creation? Does God's salvation, understood as liberation, reach as far as the cosmos? Second, if Jesus came to restore Israel, and if early Christians proclaimed the actualization of the new exodus in the coming of Jesus and the outpouring of the Spirit, what are we to make of the status of God's people in the Roman Empire? If God's dominion has drawn near, why does the empire still stand? Both questions are of interest as we make our way through the witness of scripture on salvation. They also have immediate repercussions for how we understand the place of God's people in the world, not least in a world occupied by kingdoms and governments whose laws and practices today do not align themselves with the ancient purposes of God.

Is proclamation of Yahweh the liberator good news not only for human beings but also for the cosmos? That such a question could even be raised is evidence already that something has gone wrong. As we have seen in chapter 1, the witness of scripture is that one of the first words that must be spoken over humanity concerns its inseparable, nonnegotiable relation to the world within which the human family has been created and which it inhabits. This suggests already that there are no glad tidings for the human creature that are not also good news for all of creation.

Such categories of thought do not come easily, however, at least not to people who for millennia have understood the world above all in relation to themselves, and especially to people in the United States who have long parsed the human race even further according to a bias toward individual dignity and responsibility. In their classic account of the American middle class, *Habits of the Heart*, Robert Bellah and his research team identified "autonomous individualism" as the defining quality of American life. Their account of American life would accord privilege to definitions of salvation that have to do with "finding yourself," with gaining independence, with my "pulling myself up by my own bootstraps"—or, as they put it, by freedom through mobility and detachment from social obligation.[12] Of course, it ought immediately to be acknowledged that the analysis on display in *Habits of the Heart* has

[12]Robert N. Bellah et al., *Habits of the Heart: Individualism and Commitment in American Life* (Berkeley, Calif.: Univ. of California Press, 1985); see further, *idem*, eds., *Individualism and Commitment in American Life: Readings on the Themes of "Habits of the Heart"* (San Francisco: Harper & Row, 1987).

been critiqued for giving insufficient attention to minority traditions within the United States—African American communities, for example, or the influences of feminism;[13] and, in any case, someone might ask, Has not the autonomous individualism of the mid- and late-twentieth century given way to new emphases on community with the rise of postmodernism? On the one hand, although it is true that minority movements have brought to the American table community-valuing interests and practices, it is not clear that those commitments have been heard and there is plenty of evidence that they have been and continue to be in danger of being overwhelmed by the majority culture. For example, Suzanne Gordon has lamented the degree to which the commitments of the women's movement to relationships, interdependence, collaboration, and community have gone the way of individualism and hierarchy. "Transformative feminism" has been eclipsed by the "economic woman," characterized by competition and self-interest. "We have entered the male kingdom," she writes, "and yet we have been forced to play by the king's rules."[14] Paralleling these developments is the tragic fragmentation of African American communities, and it is surely of interest that, in a highly significant collection of essays written by leading African American biblical scholars on the role of African American experience in biblical interpretation, the importance of the location of biblical study within the church as the community of God's people, for the reframing and refashioning of biblical interpretation, is not a pervasive concern.[15] A counter-example is found in Justo González' Santa Biblia: The Bible through Hispanic Eyes, which locates biblical interpretation squarely and profoundly in the Latino/Latina community as a hermeneutical presupposition;[16] the question remains whether the church in America will learn anew from its Hispanic brothers and sisters its own birthright and mandate as the community of God's people.

[13]Cf. C.H. Reynolds and R.V. Norman, eds., Community in America: The Challenge of "Habits of the Heart" (Berkeley, Calif.: Univ. of California Press, 1988).

[14]Suzanne Gordon, Prisoners of Men's Dreams: Striking out for a New Feminine Future (Boston: Little, Brown, 1991), 4.

[15]Cain Hope Felder, ed., Stony the Road We Trod: African American Biblical Interpretation (Minneapolis: Fortress Press, 1991).

[16]Justo L. González, Santa Biblia: The Bible through Hispanic Eyes (Nashville: Abingdon Press, 1996). For a broader emphasis on community in American-Hispanic theological reflection, see Miguel H. Díaz, On Being Human: U.S. Hispanic and Rahnerian Perspectives (Maryknoll, N.Y.: Orbis, 2001); Ismael García, Dignidad: Ethics through Hispanic Eyes (Nashville: Abingdon Press, 1997).

If we were to take seriously how significant our social interactions are in the formation of our "selves," right down to the formation of processes involved in the cooperative interactions within our brain systems,[17] we would not be surprised that the autonomous individualism espoused and embodied in the dominant American culture spreads like a virus into and within America's subcultures. We come to embody the influences nearest to us. Some might point to portrayals of community and friendship on primetime television's popularly rated sitcoms ("Seinfeld" or "Friends," for example) as evidence that the tide is turning; after all, these media products arguably both express and shape the imagination and practices of their viewers. Still others might point to heightened interest among Americans in the small group movement, which in 1994 was reported to involve some forty percent of the population. Although they underscore the human yearning for community, these phenomena do not signal a radical departure from earlier decades. Rather, the "community" they represent is characterized better by its breadth than its depth. This "community" places few demands on its "members," who are more likely to control their sense and experience of community than to become subjected to related commitments and obligations; and movement from friend to friend, group to group, comes with relative ease, in the service of a self-serve, do-it-yourself "community life."[18]

Undoubtedly, it is difficult to think of good news for the redemption of the cosmos when salvation is defined in terms so fully human and individual. But, again, this admission is less a commentary on the biblical portrait of divine liberation, and more a commentary on human proclivities on this side of Eden. Without neglecting the importance of an emphasis on the *personal* aspects of God's liberating power, then, we must push further by recognizing, on the one hand, that human beings are embedded in the human community and the life of the human community is embedded in the whole cosmos; and, on the other, that the forces of evil that must be overcome in salvation have targeted the whole of God's good creation, and not only individual humans.

---

[17]Cf. Joseph LeDoux, *Synaptic Self: How Our Brains Become Who We Are* (New York: Viking Press, 2002).

[18]See Robert Wuthnow, *Sharing the Journey: Support Groups and America's New Quest for Community* (New York: Free Press, 1994).

Already latent in the exodus tradition is ancient testimony in Israel's scriptures that God's people have long been aware of these larger forces requiring Yahweh's attention. The God of Israel is portrayed in Exodus as sovereign over the world's powerful structures aligned against God's purpose, seeking and shaping new structures within which God's aims and character are incarnate. As interpreted elsewhere in the scriptures, Genesis 3 already testifies to the presence of a most potent enemy against God's purposes. This is the serpent, whose introduction into the story disrupts creation harmony and leads to enmity within the human family and conflict in the cosmos (Gen. 3:1–15). In the Christian Bible's last book, this serpent is unmistakably identified as the devil, Satan, whose utter defeat is set within the framework of the coming of the day of salvation:

> And war broke out in heaven; Michael and his angels fought against the dragon. The dragon and his angels fought back, but they were defeated, and there was no longer any place for them in heaven. The great dragon was thrown down, that ancient serpent, who is called the Devil and Satan, the deceiver of the whole world—he was thrown down to the earth, and his angels were thrown down with him. Then I heard a loud voice in heaven, proclaiming,
>
> "Now have come the salvation and the power
>   and the kingdom of our God
>   and the authority of his Messiah,
> for the accuser of our comrades has been thrown down,
>   who accuses them day and night before our God."
>   (Rev. 12:7–10)

This interpretation is not a New Testament novelty, but is anticipated in Isaiah's vision of the new creation: "The wolf and the lamb shall feed together, the lion shall eat straw like the ox; but the serpent—its food shall be dust! They shall not hurt or destroy on all my holy mountain, says the LORD" (Isa. 65:25). In another Isaianic text, the demise of the serpent is correlated with an important motif from the exodus-story—namely, Yahweh's authority over the sea as an image of the conquest of evil. In Exodus, Israel's enemies "sank like lead in the mighty waters" (Ex. 15:10), whereas in Isaiah the prophet declares of the coming day of salvation, "On that day the

LORD with his cruel and great and strong sword will punish Leviathan the fleeing serpent, Leviathan the twisting serpent, and he will kill the dragon that is in the sea" (Isa. 27:1). The conflict between Yahweh and the sea, and between Yahweh and the monsters of the sea, is an often-repeated motif in Israel's scriptures. Yahweh overcomes the sea's potency through rebuke (Nah. 1:4), sits in conquest over the flood (Ps. 29:10), and has crushed the heads of Leviathan (Ps. 74:12–17; cf. Isa 27:1). It is little wonder, then, that John the Seer writes of the coming of the new creation and final conquest of evil with these words: "Then I saw a new heaven and a new earth; for the first heaven and the first earth had passed away, *and the sea was no more*" (Rev. 21:1).

It is within this frame of reference that we grasp the significance of other stories in scripture, such as the gospel accounts of Jesus walking on the water. For example, in Mark 6:45–51, we read:

> Immediately he made his disciples get into the boat and go on ahead to the other side, to Bethsaida, while he dismissed the crowd. After saying farewell to them, he went up on the mountain to pray. When evening came, the boat was out on the sea, and he was alone on the land. When he saw that they were straining at the oars against an adverse wind, he came towards them early in the morning, walking on the sea. He intended to pass them by. But when they saw him walking on the sea, they thought it was a ghost and cried out; for they all saw him and were terrified. But immediately he spoke to them and said, "Take heart, it is I; do not be afraid." Then he got into the boat with them and the wind ceased. (Author's translation)

If our categories of thought are not determined by the echoes of Israel's scriptures in this text, we might label this story a "nature miracle," or wonder at this early form of levitation. Note, however, the explicit time element ("early in the morning"), an allusion to the "morning watch" in Exodus 14:24, which marked the onset of Israel's crossing of the sea; the parallel description of the crossing of the sea in Psalm 77, which describes the waters as trembling at the sight of God, God's leading Israel by taking a path on the mighty waters ("yet your footprints were unseen"); the analogy of Jesus' intention to "pass them by" with God's "passing by" Moses (Ex. 34:6); and Jesus' self-identification with the words, "it is I" ("I am"), echoing the "I AM" of

Yahweh's self-disclosure to Moses at the burning bush (Ex. 3:14). Note, too, the scriptural testimony to Yahweh's power over chaos, expressed by control of the waters, walking on the waters, trampling the waves, overcoming its fury, and rescuing people from the sea (for example, Gen. 1:2, 6–9; 8:1–3; Job 9:8; Hab. 3:15; Pss. 18:16; 77:19; 107:23–32; Isa. 43:16; 51:9–10; Jonah 1). In short, reports of Jesus walking on the water present Jesus in the role of liberator from the chaos of evil and as the one through whom new creation is being actualized.

Of course, the portrait of Jesus in battle against the powers of evil extends further in the gospels, especially to his engagement with Satan and demons. Stories of Jesus' temptation in the wilderness and accounts of exorcism are found in the gospels of Matthew, Mark, and Luke.[19] An important window into the significance of these accounts is provided by the controversy over Jesus' association with Beelzebul in Luke 11:17–22:

> But he knew what they were thinking and said to them, "Every kingdom divided against itself becomes a desert, and house falls on house. If Satan also is divided against himself, how will his kingdom stand?—for you say that I cast out the demons by Beelzebul. Now if I cast out the demons by Beelzebul, by whom do your exorcists cast them out? Therefore they will be your judges. But if it is by the finger of God that I cast out the demons, then the kingdom of God has come to you. When a strong man, fully armed, guards his castle, his property is safe. But when one stronger than he attacks him and overpowers him, he takes away his armor in which he trusted and divides his plunder."

What is at stake in this exchange is the source of Jesus' authority. The charge brought against him, "He casts out demons by Beelzebul, the ruler of the demons" (Lk. 11:15), acknowledges Jesus' success as an exorcist, but attempts to marginalize Jesus' influence among the people by casting him in the role of a magician, or witch—that is, a social and religious deviant not to be taken seriously. Jesus' response

---

[19]Mt. 4:1–11; Mk. 1:13; Lk. 4:1–13; and also Mt. 11:2–6; 12:22–30; Mk. 1:21–28; 3:22–27; 5:1–20; 7:24–30; 9:14–29; Lk. 7:18–23; 11:14–23; 13:10–17. Among recent treatments, see Sydney H.T. Page, *Powers of Evil: A Biblical Study of Satan and Demons* (Grand Rapids, Mich.: Baker, 1995); Graham H. Twelftree, *Jesus the Exorcist: A Contribution to the Study of the Historical Jesus* (Peabody, Mass.: Hendrickson, 1993).

presumes (1) that the names "Beelzebul" ("Lord of the Flies") and "Satan" refer to the same entity; (2) Satan is the head of a household or kingdom; (3) Satan exercises command over demons, who serve his aim; and (4) the unity of Satan's dominion. Consequently, if Jesus were to wield the authority of Satan, this would signal Satan's countenancing civil war within his own domain, an absurdity. Instead, Jesus insists, his exorcisms bring to tangible expression a stronger power than that brandished by the Lord of the Flies; they are manifestations of God's own power, the sovereignty of God breaking into the world by means of the ministry of Jesus. "The finger of God" refers to God's active power, especially as displayed in the exodus-tradition. Faced with the plagues brought against Egypt, Pharaoh's magicians exclaim, "This is the finger of God!" (Ex. 8:19). In the same way, Jesus' exorcisms are manifestations of the power of the liberating God, who sets free those who have been bound by Satan (cf. Lk. 13:10–17). If, as Jesus' ministry of exorcism portends, "the kingdom of God has come to you," then the dominion of Satan is being repealed.

Turning from Jesus to Paul, we turn from this sort of direct engagement with diabolic power to numerous references to "principalities and powers," a phrase Paul uses to refer to powers aligned against the purpose of God and, thus, against Christ and his church. Actually, Paul deploys a range of related terms: "principalities," "rulers," "authorities," "powers," "dominions," "thrones," "angels," and "cosmic rulers of this darkness," to name the more prominent.[20] What these terms denote is not always certain, though in Pauline usage they typically refer to spiritual forces that come to expression in socio-political realities. That is, only rarely, if ever, can one attribute to Paul a concern with spiritual forces of evil devoid of their expression in human institutions; and neither can one attribute to Paul a theology of human institutions aligned against God that does not account for the animation of those institutions with diabolic breath. In the world of Paul, popular religion, associated with magic, mystery, and astrology, concocted a world inhabited by spirits capable of being manipulated to achieve ends both good and evil. Spiritual powers, then, were often regarded as malevolent, to be feared and, whenever possible, appeased. Paul does not deny the existence of "powers and principalities," but he does put them in their place. (See especially

---

[20]Cf. Daniel G. Reid, "Principalities and Powers," in *Dictionary of Paul and His Letters,* ed. Gerald F. Hawthorne, Ralph P. Martin, and Daniel G. Reid (Downers Grove, Ill.: InterVarsity, 1993), 746–52 (748–49).

Col. 1—2.) First, they should not be regarded as eternal. Since they were created through Christ, they were inhabitants of a created cosmos over which God could pronounce the verdict, "It is good." The details of the narrative are missing in Paul, but it is clear nonetheless that the powers had failed to exercise their assigned role in the cosmos, and had become hostile to God's purposes and people. Nevertheless, he affirms, in the cross of Christ, the powers had been unmasked in their pretensions to royal authority and grandeur. Stripped of the garments of their dominion, the powers were not annihilated but restored to their purpose in creation. Having been conquered in Jesus' death, they had been reconciled to Christ. Borrowing language from the exodus story, Paul sketches this process of reconciliation in terms of deliverance: "He has rescued us from the power of darkness and transferred us into the kingdom of his beloved Son, in whom we have redemption, the forgiveness of sins" (Col. 1:13–14). Indeed, the images tumble over one another in this text, so that salvation is represented as divine rescue both from the shackles of an evil dominion aligned against God and from the dire consequences of our sinful acts, and as the anticipation of the restoration of creation.

Without in any way wishing to undermine the concrete realities of the liberation Paul thus sketches, it is also true that Paul understands liberation as having an essentially hermeneutical value. That is, God's people are those who have passed from one way of construing the cosmos to another, so that they are able to see with the eyes of faith the astounding presence of God at work in the world and to reconsider the value they place on the constituents of that world. For example, in Galatians 4:3, 9, Paul refers to a much-contested phrase, "the elements of the cosmos" (author's translation; cf. NRSV's "elemental spirits"). If we take this phrase in its most simple sense, it refers to the basic elements of the world—in the philosophical thought of his day, to the fourfold opposition of air/earth, fire/water, cold/hot, wet/dry. If we take into account the socio-religious world as this had been defined in Paul's letter to the Galatians, these oppositions would be Jew/Gentile, slave/free, male/female (Gal. 3:28). Here, then, would be an instance of transformation, not only in the referent of "elements of the cosmos," but, more crucially, with regard to the basic way in which the world is defined.[21] With the advent of Christ, and with the

[21]Cf. J. Louis Martyn, *Theological Issues in the Letters of Paul* (Nashville: Abingdon Press, 1997), 125–40.

appropriation of the work of Christ in Christian baptism, the elements of social and religious distinction are reinterpreted. "There is no longer Jew or Greek, there is no longer slave or free, there is no longer male and female; for all of you are one in Christ Jesus" (Gal. 3:28). Similarly, "From now on, therefore, we regard no one from a human point of view; even though we once knew Christ from a human point of view, we know him no longer in that way. So if anyone is in Christ, there is a new creation: everything old has passed away; see, everything has become new!" (2 Cor. 5:16–17).

For some, words about liberation and rescue in the New Testament may sound rather hollow, since, when they were first spoken or written in the first century, they appear not to have manifested themselves in proactive resistance against the Roman Empire. How could those first Christians speak of divine deliverance without dealing immediately and forcefully with Rome, whose imperial life stood in conspicuous opposition to the aims of God and the commitments of God's people? If exodus from Egyptian oppression is the paradigm for God's intervention, what does it mean to proclaim a new exodus if not deliverance from Roman oppression? Let me mention two ways of addressing this question.

First, we must recognize how the terms of the exodus have been transformed. Previously, the line between Israel and its enemies seems to have been more easily drawn: the Hebrew people on the one side, their Egyptian oppressors on the other. The tenets of Torah complicated this somewhat, by extending the care and compassion of Yahweh and, therefore, of Israel, also to the alien that lived among God's people. Stories in Israel's scriptures demonstrate further how God's mercy and healing extended beyond the borders of Israel—to Naaman the Syrian leper, for example, or to the Sidonian widow—stories that provide a pattern for Jesus' ministry in Luke's gospel (1 Kings 17:8–24; 2 Kings 5:1–19; Lk. 4:16–30). The tale of Jonah is indicative of how easily, and erroneously, those outside the boundaries of Israel might be regarded as the enemy. Indeed, God must go to extraordinary ends to convince Jonah of the reach of God's compassion and of the capacity of those beyond the boundaries of God's people to hear God's word and respond appropriately: "Should I not be concerned about Nineveh, that great city, in which there are more than a hundred and twenty thousand persons who do not know their right hand from their left, and also many animals?" (Jon. 4:11). In the dim light of only the most stark of prophetic warnings, "Forty days more, and Nineveh shall be overthrown!" (Jon. 3:4), both humans and animals mourn and repent (Jon. 3:5–10). The irony of Nineveh's response is not lost on Jesus, who declares to God's own people, Israel, "The people of Nineveh will rise up at the judgment with this generation and condemn it, because they repented at the proclamation of Jonah, and see, something greater than Jonah is here!" (Lk. 11:32).

"Who is my neighbor?" the legal expert asks of Jesus, in the midst of their exchange on the implications of Leviticus 19:18: "You shall love your neighbor as yourself." That neighborly relations of compassion would extend to Jew-Samaritan relations, who could have anticipated? And yet this is the position Jesus takes in his parable of the Good Samaritan (Lk. 10:25–37), a position that he regards as fully congruent with Torah. Similarly, Paul recognizes that Gentiles could no longer be cast straightforwardly as enemies, since the death of Christ had razed the old dividing walls and opened the way for a single human family in Christ (for example, Gal. 3:10–14; cf. Col. 1:21; Eph. 2:17). The heavenly gathering of God's people, John reports, includes persons "from every nation, from all tribes and peoples and languages" (Rev. 7:9–11). Clearly, the line between "us" and "them" has become more difficult to manage or maintain, or even draw.

For our present discussion, a far-reaching effect of this transformation is a depersonalization of the concept of "enemy." The true enemy of God's people could not be identified with the people of Rome, but rather with the forces and powers that found expression in Roman rule. An important consequence is a shift of battleground, from flesh-and-blood hostility to a confrontation over what values, what allegiances, what interpretations of the world, would govern the commitments and behaviors of God's people.

Second, then, we must take seriously the multitudinous ways in which the pages of the New Testament are subversive of the Roman Empire, of Roman rule, of Roman religion, of Roman ideology. Because the New Testament writers do not generally call for outright revolutionary resistance, they have sometimes been thought to promote a pro-Roman stance. Nothing could be further from the truth,[22] as these examples will suggest:

[22]See, e.g., Walter E. Pilgrim, *Uneasy Neighbors: Church and State in the New Testament*, Overtures to Biblical Theology (Minneapolis: Fortress Press, 1999); Richard J. Cassidy, *Christians and Roman Rule in the New Testament: New Perspectives*, Companions to the New Testament (New York: Crossroad, 2001).

- The birth of Jesus as narrated by Luke sets in contrast two ways of peace, two kingdoms (Lk. 2:1–20).[23] On the one hand is Roman peace—celebrated as "good news," lodged in worldwide recognition of Caesar Augustus as the savior of Rome and lord of all civilized peoples, expressed by and enforced in the business of census-taking, itself the necessary precursor to exacting yearly taxes from a subjugated people. On the other hand is Jesus, "Savior" and "Lord," whose birth is celebrated as the "good news" that signals the advent of peace that comes from "highest heaven." In the context of Imperial Rome, Mary's Song in Luke 1:46–55 takes on a more threatening and revolutionary tone: "He has brought down the powerful from their thrones, and lifted up the lowly; he has filled the hungry with good things, and sent the rich away empty."

- For Paul, the lordship of Christ is an enormously significant *political* statement. In a world in which Gentile kings "lord it over" their subjects, and "those in authority…are called benefactors" (Lk. 22:25), Paul's christology has special poignancy. In Philippians, for example, Jesus' lordship is universal (so that lord Nero, too, would bow, confessing that Jesus Christ is Lord) and grounded in his humbling himself and becoming obedient unto death, indeed, in his embracing the ignominy of death by crucifixion (Phil. 2:6–11). On this basis, Paul can argue throughout his letter to the Philippians that they are to take their standards for comportment in the Empire from Lord Jesus and not from lord emperor (for example, Phil. 1:27–30).

- In an apparently innocuous list of prescribed attitudes, Peter writes, "Honor everyone. Love the family of believers. Fear God. Honor the emperor" (1 Pet. 2:17). In a world determined by Roman hegemony, the last admonition, "Honor the emperor," is expected, a reflection of the increasingly pervasive influence of the worship of the emperor as though he were a god. Juxtaposing this admonition with the universal counsel, "Honor everyone," undercuts the cult of the emperor by leveling the playing field, however. The emperor is to be

---

[23]See Joel B. Green, *The Gospel of Luke,* New International Commentary on the New Testament (Grand Rapids, Mich.: Wm. B. Eerdmans, 1997), 120–38.

honored not as a deity, separate from and above all other persons, but, simply, along with all other persons, because he is a member of the human family.

• One last example: In Revelation, John divulges the contents of a Rome-bound seafaring cargo in order to portray the center of the Empire as a mistress-harlot who maintains a luxurious lifestyle at the expense of her lovers, the conquered peoples of the Roman empire. He thus exposes a network of economic interests—including kings, merchants, and mariners, who have most to gain from Roman economic dominance; as well as common subjects, exploited but bedazzled by Roman opulence and propaganda. This cargo record consists of "gold, silver, jewels and pearls, fine linen, purple, silk and scarlet, all kinds of scented wood, all articles of ivory, all articles of costly wood, bronze, iron, and marble, cinnamon, spice, incense, myrrh, frankincense, wine, olive oil, choice flour and wheat, cattle and sheep, horses and chariots, slaves—and human lives" (18:12–13). Where the NRSV reads "slaves—and human lives," the Greek text might better be translated "bodies—even the souls of humans" or "bodies—that is, human lives." That is, the NRSV masks the reduction of "slaves" to "bodies" in this ocean-going manifest, a reductionism that provides evidence of Rome's debasement of human beings. Even slaves are more than their physicality; they are human beings wrongly catalogued by their materiality, like so many carcasses, alongside cattle and sheep.

These are subtle, but real, illustrations of the way the gospel would erode the seemingly impregnable strongholds of Roman ideology. Read through the lens provided by the biblical witness to Yahweh as liberator, such texts remind us that the message of the exodus continues into and beyond the New Testament.

Epilogue

Many of the threads of this discussion come together in Revelation, the last book of the Bible. This may be expected, since in so many ways the books of Genesis and Revelation form a matching set of bookends to the Christian scriptures, with new creation embracing and extending creation. Our interest in Yahweh the liberator comes into particular focus in Revelation, with its major development of the motifs of war and conquest. It is not too much to say that Revelation is the Bible's most violent book, with images of combat, battle, and triumph splashed across almost every page. At the conclusion of this discussion of salvation as liberation for the whole cosmos, including the people of God, it will be helpful to explore these images briefly, not least given the role this prophetic book gives to the people of God in the last battle.

The importance of the cosmos to the revolutionary message of salvation of Revelation is signaled in several ways. First, in the opening scene of John's vision, located in heaven's great throne room, God is celebrated as Creator:

> You are worthy, our Lord and God
>   to receive glory and honor and power,
> for you created all things,
>   and by your will they existed and were created.
>   (Rev 4:11)

That is, God's saving purpose and intervention is set within the larger framework of the whole of creation. This is fully congruent with Israel's expectation that the time of restoration would not be concentrated narrowly on the salvation of individuals, nor even on humanity; Israel's hope was for the restoration of the whole of God's creation.

Indeed, this is the reality to which John's vision would point: "Then I saw a new heaven and a new earth; for the first heaven and the first earth had passed away, and the sea was no more" (Rev. 21:1). Continuity between the present and future is guaranteed by the dual mention of heaven and earth. Discontinuity is signaled by the repetition of the adjective "new," which here, as in the Judaism of the first century, might better be translated as "renewed." It is "new" in the sense that cosmic restoration requires the fresh, creative work of God, but not in the sense that the old is discarded so as to be replaced by an altogether different creation. "See," the Creator proclaims, "I am making all things new" (Rev. 21:5), using words that echo the promise of renewal in Isaiah 65:17 and that cast the work of salvation on a mural of the grandest of proportions, the whole cosmos.

Second, and perhaps more noticeable, is how John has portrayed the character of evil in Revelation. At times, it may appear that Rome is the axis of evil in the world John paints, but it is significant that

Rome, also known as Babylon, is not the target of divine warfare. God's people are to abandon Rome, but are not called to work for its destruction (Rev. 18:4). The principal enemy of God, the enemy that must be defeated, is that diabolic triad: the dragon or serpent, the deceiver of the world, the devil, or Satan (Rev. 12:9; 11:18; 20:2); the sea-beast, which exercises the dominion of the dragon (Rev. 13:1– 10); and the earth-beast, which causes people to worship the sea-beast (Rev. 13:11–18). Within the world John portrays, the sea-beast is none other than the imperial dominion of Rome, which exerts itself over against the purposes of God and makes for itself the claim of possessing and exercising exalted, absolute power. Given our earlier comments on the association of the sea with chaos and evil, it is no wonder that John envisions the dragon as calling this beast out of the sea, nor that Rome has extended its power in large part through its control of the Mediterranean. It would have been by the sea that Rome first made its presence and power known to the lands of the East, including the territories to which John has addressed his book. Similarly, the earth-beast would refer to those varied means by which the worship of Rome and Rome's leader would have spread throughout the Empire. In other words, the battle between good and evil does not pit Christians against non-believers; rather, this confrontation is cosmic in its scale, with divine energies arrayed against the powers lurking behind and guiding the human faces of this world's empires.

For John, a chief symbol of salvation is the exodus, with Jesus himself presented as the Passover Lamb through whom the forces of evil are overcome and God's people are ransomed and gathered as "a kingdom and priests serving our God" (Rev. 5; cf. Ex. 19:5–6). Combining references to the exodus and to Isaiah's new exodus, John shows that the liberating roles of Passover Lamb and Suffering Servant of Isaiah converge in the sacrificial death of Jesus. Other images from Exodus abound: Christian martyrs who have experienced the new exodus, crossed the heavenly Red Sea and stand at its banks singing the Song of Moses (Rev. 15:1–5), for example, and the series of plagues by which God judges those who oppose God's will (Rev. 15—16).

What is the role of God's people in the battle? John attributes victory to the Lion and the Lamb, both references to Christ, in Revelation 5:5; 17:14. More pervasive, however, is the designation of God's faithful as those who conquer (for example, Rev. 2:7, 11, 17, 26; 15:2; 21:7), which identifies them immediately as personally engaged in the conflict. On the one hand, this means that quiet acquiescence and withdrawal are not among the options available to God's people as they seek a faithful response to the presence of evil in the world. On the other, it presses the importance of identifying clearly and exercising faithfully the implements of war. In our interaction with Revelation, a book seemingly overrun with images of violence, this is all the more crucial, and Revelation 12:11 is thematic in this respect: "They have conquered him by the blood of the Lamb and by the word of their testimony, for they did not cling to life even in the face of death." God's people are called to overcome the enemy, but not with artillery taken from the arsenal of any earthly military machine. Instead, the weapons of their conquest are patient endurance and faithfulness (2:3, 7, 10, 11, 25, 26; 3:5, 12; 13:10; 14:12; 15:2), and the blood of the Lamb and the testimony of the word (12:11; 19:10). That is, the divine war against evil is engaged and won through our adopting the way of the Lamb, through our active participation as witnesses to the truth of God, even at the cost of our lives. "To be faithful to the true God even to the point of death is not to become a victim of the beast, but to take the field against him and win."[24]

John thus underscores for us the radical character of evil, together with the even more momentous power of God. Conquering is costly, and demands a rebirth of images that will allow us to imagine that faithful witness in life and death has unrivaled and irrepressible potency in the face of evil. The chorus sung to the Lamb of God draws on exodus-memory to remind us of the topsy-turvy way Yahweh the liberator actualizes God's purpose:

"You are worthy to take the scroll
    and to open its seals,
for you were slaughtered and by your blood you
        ransomed for God
    saints from every tribe and language and people
        and nation;
you have made them to be a kingdom and priests
        serving our God,
    and they will reign on earth." (Rev. 5:9–10)

---

[24]Richard Bauckham, *The Theology of the Book of Revelation,* New Testament Theology (Cambridge: Cambridge Univ. Press, 1993), 91.

4

HOW CAN WE BE SAVED?

"**S**ave yourselves from this corrupt generation." These words form a précis of Peter's prophetic address to those gathered at Pentecost, as Luke narrates the story (Acts 2:40). Resident in these words we find both puzzle and perplexity—the one baffling, the other haunting.

The enigma lies in the apparent assertion that persons in Peter's audience ought to "save themselves"—that is, that they are capable of saving themselves, that they might be the agents of their own deliverance. It is possible to translate the verb differently, as a passive, so that it reads, "Be saved!" It is precisely at the point of navigating these options that we are caught short, however, since throughout scripture these two are held in tandem: the identification of God alone as Savior and the invitation of God for partners in the way of salvation. We find in scripture requests that God save (for example, 1 Sam. 7:8; 2 Kings 19:9; 1 Chr. 16:35), as well as ample evidence that people can serve as God's agents to bring salvation to others (for example, 1 Sam. 24—26), but even these texts make clear that salvation nonetheless belongs to the Lord. That is, salvation is not ours to accomplish, but has as its consistent subject God, and yet this does not relegate human beings to roles of mere passivity.

Herein lies the haunting perplexity: Since human beings cannot adopt a merely passive role in the face of God's work of salvation, human response is necessary. And Peter's prophetic warning presumes that the divine work of salvation can be embraced as well as resisted. Moreover, his reference to "this corrupt generation" presumes that God's saving design actually will be resisted. Salvation is clearly available, but the announcement of good news doubles as a pronouncement of pending division within Israel. (See Lk. 2:34–35.) As was the case with Israel in the exodus-story, so is the case with some at the onset of the new exodus; people can and will respond to God's saving initiative perversely, rebelliously (Ex. 32:9; 33:3; Deut. 10:16; 32:5; cf. Lk. 11:29–32, 47–51; 17:25; Acts 7:51–53). Salvation, therefore, entails no less than disassociating from that group of corrupt grumblers, through responses of faith, repentance, and baptism (Acts 2:38).

We have already seen important evidence of the biblical identification of God as Savior—that is, as the subject of the work and initiator of salvation—in our chapters on Yahweh as healer and liberator. This central point can be further pressed by taking seriously the background in Israel's scriptures of the central Christian concern with the "gospel." Since the days of Justin Martyr (ca. 100–165 C.E.), Christians have known the first four books of the New Testament as "gospels," and so have learned to associate the term with narratives of the ministry, death, and resurrection of Jesus. For Paul, and in Christian proclamation more generally, the "gospel" is the word of truth (Col. 1:5), the word of reconciliation (2 Cor. 5:19), the word of salvation (Eph. 1:13), the word of the cross (1 Cor. 1:18), the transforming word, which has Jesus Christ as its object and source. Yet, this is the "gospel" that New Testament authors also know as "the gospel of God,"[1] and which shares its linguistic and conceptual genotype with announcements of glad tidings in Israel's scriptures (that is, the Septuagint). There, and especially in Isaiah, this gospel is the good news of end-time salvation marked by the return of Yahweh's presence. "Strengthen the weak hands, and make firm the feeble knees. Say to those who are of a fearful heart, 'Be strong, do not fear! *Here is your*

---

[1]Cf. Mk. 1:14; Acts 20:24; Rom. 1:1; 15:16; 2 Cor. 11:7; 1 Thess. 2:2, 8, 9; 1 Tim. 1:11; 1 Pet. 4:17.

God. He will come with vengeance, with terrible recompense. He will come and save you'" (Isa. 35:3–4, author's emphasis). Indeed, this is the wilderness cry of Isaiah's messenger of consolation: "Here is your God!" (Isa. 40:9).

> How beautiful upon the mountains
>> are the feet of the messenger who announces peace,
> who brings good news,
>> who announces salvation,
>> who says to Zion, "Your God reigns."
> Listen! Your sentinels lift up their voices,
>> together they sing for joy;
> for in plain sight they see
>> the return of the LORD to Zion. (Isa. 52:7–8)

The advent of the Lord inaugurates the deliverance of God's people from their exile among the nations. God will lead them through the waters and the fire as through the sea; God will shepherd and provision them, and they will behold God's glory. Yahweh will again make a home among the people, enthroned on Zion in a restored Jerusalem.[2] The coming of Yahweh entails salvation. Without God's return, apart from God's presence, there is no salvation.

If the biblical witness is clear in its identification of Yahweh as the source, the author of salvation, the question remains how salvation is mediated to and embraced by human beings. This is the concern of this chapter. Taking as our point of departure the witness of scripture that Yahweh draws near to save, we will first explore three "moments" in the life of Israel where the saving presence of God is on display. This agenda will turn our focus first, and briefly, to Exodus—briefly since Exodus was so central to our interests in the preceding chapter; and then to the role of the temple (and temple sacrifices) in the life of God's people and to the advent of Jesus the Savior. Following this, we will examine the sort of question asked of John the Baptist early in the gospel of Luke, and of Peter in the context of his Pentecost address: "What should we do?" (Lk. 3:10, 12, 14; Acts 2:37). Here we will explore the notion of "conversion" as response to God's gift of salvation.

---

[2]Isa. 40—55; see Rikki E. Watts, *Isaiah's New Exodus and Mark*, Wissenschaftliche Untersuchungen zum Neuen Testament 2:88 (Tübingen: J.C.B. Mohr [Paul Siebeck], 1997) 2:80–81, 88.

God Draws Near to Save

In important ways, the terms of exodus are thematic for our discussion of the mediation of salvation: Israel in need, God drawing near to save, God as a traveling companion, and the concomitant need for God's people to comport themselves as God's people. "Because the LORD your God travels along with your camp, to save you and to hand over your enemies to you, therefore your camp must be holy..." (Deut. 23:14). The presence of God distinguishes these people as God's elect, secures their liberation, and calls for them to align themselves with God's character. The Exodus account of the commission of Moses is suggestive in this regard (Ex. 3:1—4:17). Called by God to serve as the divine instrument to deliver the Israelites out of Egypt, Moses constructs one excuse after another, and each is answered with reference to God's assurance, promise, and sign. Of these, the most central is this assertion by the Lord: "Now go, and I will be with your mouth and teach you what you are to speak" (Ex. 4:12). These words, "I will be with you," are crucial.

The journey itself is replete with reminders of the divine presence: "The LORD went in front of them in a pillar of cloud by day, to lead them along the way, and in a pillar of fire by night, to give them light, so that they might travel by day and by night" (Ex. 13:21). God is present, both as leader and protector (cf. Ex. 14:19, 24). The glory of God's presence is such that it is guarded by a dense cloud (Ex. 19:9, 16). En route to the promised land, Israel proved itself a stiff-necked people, with the result that the divine presence was located outside the camp. There was the "tent of meeting," where "...the pillar of cloud would descend..., and the LORD would speak with Moses" (Ex. 33:9). When the materials for the "tabernacle of the tent of meeting" were gathered (Ex. 25—31), instructions were given for its construction; when it was finished, "then the cloud covered the tent of meeting, and the glory of the LORD filled the tabernacle" (Ex. 40:34). This was the "cloud of the LORD," which determined the daily journeying of the Exodus people. Here was the observable assurance of God's presence among the people and the place of divine revelation. (See Ex. 25:22.) Here, too, sacrifices were offered and atonement made. (See Ex. 29—30.) Just how significant this portable sanctuary was in the life shared by God and the people is suggested by the Lord's words to David, "I have not lived in a house since the day I brought up the people of Israel from Egypt to this day, but I have been moving about in a tent and a tabernacle" (2 Sam. 7:6). This is not to say that God was shackled to this earthly tent, but that God's presence in this fashion was itself constitutive of the people of Israel.

God Draws Near in the Temple

In time, the theology of divine election of God's people would be extended to the choice of Zion and the city of Jerusalem as the city of God's abode. Indeed, upon the Jerusalem temple's destruction in 587 B.C.E., the reconstruction of the temple became the centerpiece of Israel's hopes for restoration (for example, Isa. 60; Zech. 6:12–13). Given the theological importance of the temple, this is not surprising.

More than the religious center of Israel, the temple served as the locus of God's presence with the people. Between them, the phrases "house of God" and "house of the Lord" appear more than three hundred times in Israel's scriptures, bearing witness to the preeminent status of the temple as God's own place of dwelling. When this temple was made fully ready,

> "a cloud filled the house of the Lord, so that the
> priests could not stand to minister because of the
> cloud; for the glory of the Lord filled the house of
> the Lord. Then Solomon said,
> "The Lord has said that he would dwell in
> thick darkness.
> I have built you an exalted house,
> a place for you to dwell in forever."
> (1 Kings 8:10–13)

The site on which the temple was built was divinely revealed (2 Sam. 24:16; 2 Chron. 3:1; Ps. 132:13); Zion was God's own mountain (Pss. 68:17; 76:3; 78:69–70); and the presence of God at the temple signified Israel's election and security. Such was the marvel of God's presence in the temple that Israel would eventually develop a self-delusional and self-defeating confidence in the protection the temple would afford. Even in the context of their unjust practices, God's people would repeat, like a mantra, "This is the temple of the Lord, the temple of the Lord, the temple of the Lord" (Jer. 7:4). They did not recognize that, just as the glorious presence of God had descended on the temple, so could God's glory ascend from it, in response to the injustice of God's people (cf. 2 Kings 25:9; Ezek. 8—10).

As with temples that formed the center of life for other peoples, the temple played a crucial role in constructing Israel's sacred and social life.[3] Here is the meeting place between humanity and God, a site imbued with reminiscences of the Garden of Eden (cf. Ezekiel 47). The abode of God represented in its very architecture the cosmos. God's presence was accessed here, making this the center of divine illumination and revelation, of sacrifice and prayer, and, so, of worship. As one moved closer to the dwelling place of God, within the temple's courts and within the sanctuary itself, so one moved closer to the presence of God's holiness. For God's people, this called for increasing attention to purity, to religious sanctity.

The characteristic act of worship for Israel in relation to the temple was the offering of sacrifice; in fact, in Israel's scriptures, "worship is tantamount to sacrificing."[4] God's people not only rendered service to their God in this way, but also declared their humility before and dependence on God. The variety of sacrifices—burnt offering, peace offering, sin offering—and general regulations for how to perform them are found in Leviticus 1—7, though related rituals are found throughout the Pentateuch. More central to our purposes is our need to understand the significance of sacrifice, especially in terms of their efficacy in returning the people to right relationship with God.

In this respect, the most important of the sacrifices are the "sin offering" (Lev. 4:1—6:7; 6:24—7:10) and the sacrifice offered annually on Yom Kippur, the Day of Atonement (Lev. 16). In the former, the unblemished animal is presented to Yahweh as a sin offering, the priest lays his hand on the head of the bull before it is slaughtered, the blood is smeared or sprinkled on the altar, and the fat is removed and burnt upon the altar. According to the latter, once each year, the high priest presents a bull as a sin offering for himself and his kin, sprinkling the blood upon the mercy seat. After this, he slaughters the goat of the sin offering, making atonement for the holy place, on account of the sins of Israel. Then, he presents a second goat, lays his hands upon it, confesses the sins of the whole people over it, and sends it away into the wilderness. According to Leviticus 16:22, "The goat

---

[3]Cf. David M. Knipe, "The Temple in Image and Reality," in *Temple in Society,* ed. Michael V. Fox (Winona Lake, Ind.: Eisenbrauns, 1988), 105–38; Francis Schmidt, *How the Temple Thinks: Identity and Social Cohesion in Ancient Judaism,* The Biblical Seminar 78 (Sheffield: Sheffield Academic Press, 2001).

[4]Cf. Menahem Haran, "Temple and Community in Ancient Israel," in Fox, ed., *Temple in Society,* 17–25 (23).

shall bear on itself all their iniquities to a barren region; and the goat shall be set free in the wilderness."

The basic structure of how atonement "works" is sketched in Leviticus 19:22: "And the priest shall make atonement for him with the ram of guilt offering before the LORD for his sin that he committed; and the sin he committed shall be forgiven him." Human sin, in this case a man's sleeping with a female slave chosen to serve as a concubine for another, has resulted in broken relations between the sinner and God; it is this broken relationship, and not divine anger (which plays no role in this text and, actually, is mentioned only rarely), that must be overcome. Serving as mediator, the priest resolves this tension through a sacrifice—provided by the sinner but offered at the hands of the priest. As is often the case, the location of this sacrifice is noted: "before the LORD"—that is, "in the temple," the house of the Lord.

Unfortunately for contemporary readers of these texts, the scriptures of Israel never interpret the inner logic of these ritual acts. How to perform the rite is given careful attention, and it is evident that sacrificial rites are effective in restoring right relations with God. How this is so is not so clear and is never spelled out in a straightforward way. Apparently, their meaning was so obvious to those who practiced them that commentary was unnecessary. Today, however, their significance is less easy to penetrate, and scholars are not all of one mind, especially with regard to that central act wherein the priest lays his hand on the head of the animal. What does seem to be clear?[5] First, basic to the legislation regarding these rituals is the opposition of life and death—with death a great evil to be avoided, and with everything related to death (whether the corpse itself, or bloody discharge or disease) rendering people unclean and unfit to worship God. Second, the necessity for choosing unblemished animals serves as an analogy for the election of Israel, the choice of this people by God, set apart for service to God. Third, in the sacrifice, the notion of "identification" or "representation" seems fundamental. By laying hands on the beast's head in the ritual of sacrifice, sinners identified

[5]On what follows, see Gordon J. Wenham, "The Theology of Old Testament Sacrifice," in *Sacrifice in the Bible*, ed. Rogert T. Beckwith and Martin J. Selman (Grand Rapids, Mich.: Baker, 1995), 75–87; Brevard S. Childs, *Biblical Theology of the Old and New Testaments: Theological Reflection on the Christian Bible* (Minneapolis: Fortress Press, 1992), 503–7; B. Lang, "Kipper," in *Theological Dictionary of the Old Testament*, vol. 7, ed. G. Johannes Botterweck, Helmer Ringgren, and Heinz-Josef Fabry (Grand Rapids, Mich.: Wm. B. Eerdmans, 1995), 288–303.

themselves with the beast, indicating that the beast now represented sinners in their sin. The same might be said for the rituals involving blood, the sprinkling or smearing of the animal's blood on the people on whose behalf the sacrifice is made (for example, Ex. 24:8; 29:10, 15, 19–20; Lev 3:2, 8, 13; 14:14). In this instance, the shedding of blood—regarded as the substance of life, and therefore sacred to God—signifies the offering of the lives of those for whom the sacrifice is made. In God's economy, Israelites were thus to do to their animals what they were not allowed to do to their children or themselves; animal life substitutes for human life, and this had efficacy in the restoration of right relations with God.[6]

God Draws Near in the Advent of Jesus

It is against this backdrop that central motifs of the presentation of Jesus in the New Testament will come to have obvious significance. According to the opening of John's Gospel, the "Word" that was "with God," "was God," and through whom "all things came into being," the "Word" that is identified with Jesus, "became flesh and lived among us, and we have seen his glory" (Jn. 1:1–14). The term "lived" can more precisely be translated with reference to "pitching his tent," or "making camp," a transparent reference to the experience of the exodus-people, among whom the glory of God was seen in the pillar of cloud that would descend upon the tent of meeting. Early on in John's gospel, Jesus is acknowledged as "the Lamb of God who takes away the sin of the world!" (Jn. 1:29), an identification of Jesus as the Passover sacrifice. Shortly thereafter, Jesus identifies himself with the temple—destroyed and, after three days, rebuilt (Jn. 3:19–20). To mention only one further example, in the book of Hebrews, we find the image of Jesus as the perfect sacrificial victim positioned side by side with a portrait of Jesus as the high priest who offers the perfect sacrifice. As the perfect priest and the perfect sacrifice, Jesus obviates the need for additional sacrificial offerings (for example, Heb. 9:25–28; 10:10, 12–14). In these and plentiful other ways, the writings of the New Testament reflect on the life, death, and resurrection of Jesus in relation to God's presence, and thus as the means by which God draws near to save.

---

[6]See James D.G. Dunn, "Paul's Understanding of the Death of Jesus as Sacrifice," in *Sacrifice and Redemption: Durham Essays in Theology*, ed. S.W. Sykes (Cambridge: Cambridge Univ. Press, 1991), 35–56.

Jesus, Savior

If anything, the importance of the temple only intensified in the years surrounding the birth of Jesus. Though the temple built under Solomon was razed in 587 B.C.E., this edifice (or, rather, a poor facsimile of it) was rebuilt toward the end of the sixth century B.C.E. It was then significantly reconstructed and expanded under Herod the Great beginning in the late first century B.C.E. The Herodian temple to which Jesus would have been brought as an infant for dedication (Lk. 2:22–38), and which would be destroyed in the Jewish War (66–70 C.E.), extended over some thirty-five acres and was regarded as one of the wonders of the world. The words of Jesus' disciples with reference to the temple, "Look, Teacher, what large stones and what large buildings!" (Mk. 13:1), provide some indication of the awe in which the structure must have been held, not least among small-town Galilean folk. Jesus' reply, "Do you see these great buildings? Not one stone will be left here upon another; all will be thrown down" (Mk. 13:2), must therefore have been all the more stunning. That he thus predicted not only the fall of the temple structures themselves, but also the demise of the theology resident in them, makes his words all the more pressing.

For the Judaism of this period, known as Second Temple Judaism, the temple was the focal point of profound theological reflection. In a world of religious pluralism and syncretism, Israel's one temple in Jerusalem unified Israel under one God. And the architectural plan of the temple—which segregated priest from non-priest, Jewish male from Jewish female, Jew from Gentile, clean from unclean—sanctioned the social map that determined Israel's life. That is, the temple ordered the socio-religious world of the Jewish people, correlating Jewish belief in one God (monism) with the certain privilege of Jewish election (exclusivity). The temple's basic categories of pure and impure extended from sacrificial altar in the temple to the customary gathering at the table in Jewish homes, determining social relations and everyday behavior in Palestine and beyond. Pivotal for this temple theology was the theology of "presence": If the temple served as God's house, then honoring the temple was tantamount to honoring God and acknowledging God's presence among the people; and honoring the temple entailed living as though its structures and values of holiness and separation actually mattered in daily routines. Even among those Jews most critical of the temple, the point at issue was typically not the temple *per se* but illegitimate practices that plagued temple worship, a critique already at home in the prophetic literature of the scriptures (for example, Isa. 66:3).

The ongoing significance of the temple and its sacrificial system in the time of Jesus is important to grasp, then, not only because it helps us to understand the terrain of Jesus' life and ministry. Additionally, it provides a window into the role of the temple in ordering the life of Israel and in certifying for the Jewish people the saving presence of God in their midst. Even if the prophetic critique of the temple would continue, even if visions of the new, end-time temple would infiltrate the literature of the Second Temple period, the daily din of holy activity in Jerusalem's temple nonetheless provided powerful warrant for claims of God's blessing for Israel as well as powerful sanction for the practices and teaching of the Jewish elite in Jerusalem. If Jesus were to proclaim the restoration of Israel in this setting, he would have to address these powerful forces and the longings around which they were oriented.

Jesus and the Restoration of Israel

To insist on the importance of the temple as a tangible sign of God's blessing for Israel is not to suggest that the Jewish people of Jesus' day believed that God's promises had been fulfilled. The realities of life under Roman rule kept most from thinking in such terms. For them, the experience of exile was not a distant memory but present experience. Only the names of the pagan, overlord nations had changed: from Babylon in the sixth century B.C.E. to Rome at the turn of the era. Numerous texts of the Second Temple Period interpret Israel's lot using the language of exile and oppression, and express hopes of redemption and restoration.[7] Hence, even if in the larger Roman world, "salvation" had to do with the exercise of beneficent power for the provision of blessings, for Israel this concept was parsed in terms of Yahweh's coming to deliver Israel from the hands of its enemies and providing them security that they might serve Yahweh. God was to rescue the people from their oppressors, protect them from pressures to conform to alien ways, renew the covenant through

---

[7]This material has been helpfully surveyed in Craig A. Evans, "Jesus and the Continuing Exile of Israel," in *Jesus and the Restoration of Israel*, ed. Carey C. Newman (Downers Grove, Ill.: InterVarsity, 1999), 77–100 (esp. 78–91).

forgiving Israel's unfaithfulness, and re-gather the people under sovereign mercy.[8] The primary way in which these ideas are present in the gospels of Matthew, Mark, and Luke is in Jesus' proclamation of the kingdom of God.

To speak of the "kingdom of God" is immediately to raise the question of language. In recent decades, many have objected to the use of the word *kingdom* as possessing inherently masculine connotations, and therefore translated the Greek word *basileia* with the English word *reign* instead. This is unfortunate for two reasons. First, although it is true that *basileia* possessed hierarchical and masculine connotations in Roman antiquity, this did not keep Jesus from using the term and using it in ways that actually subverted those connotations. To say, as he did, that the "kingdom of God" belongs to little children is to militate against common understandings of the term "kingdom" in his world. Second, "kingdom" is more than "reign," for it also includes the notion of "realm," and the translation of *basileia* as "reign" too easily allows us to reduce the work of God to the "life of the spirit" or to those people among whom God reigns. In either case, the challenge of the kingdom of God has been severely curtailed. "Dominion" may be a serviceable alternative, then, in a way that "reign" cannot be.

We find more than one hundred references to the kingdom of God in the gospels, and this alone suggests its importance. We can orient ourselves to what is at stake by attending more narrowly to the appearance of this phrase in the introduction to the gospel of Mark. The boundaries of Mark's prologue are set by matching references to "gospel" in 1:1, 14–15:

"the beginning of the gospel of Jesus Christ, the Son of God, is as it was written in the prophet Isaiah" (1:1)

"Jesus came to Galilee proclaiming the gospel of God" (1:14)

"The long-awaited time has been fulfilled; the kingdom of God has drawn near. Repent and believe the gospel!" (1:15)[9]

---

[8]See, e.g., Jer. 4:14; 31:31–34; 1 Macc. 3:18–22; 4:11; 9:46; 2 Macc. 1:11, 25; 2:17–18; 7:1–42; 8:27–29; 1QM.
[9]Author's translation.

In this way, Mark tethers the significance of Jesus to the message of Isaiah. In other ways, too, Mark reads the importance of Jesus within the contours of Isaianic prophecy. Note the following parallels:

- The coming of John (compare Mk. 1:4–8 with Isa. 40)
- The baptism of Jesus (compare Mk. 1:9–11 with Isa. 42:1; 61:1)
- Jesus in the wilderness (compare Mk. 1:12–13 with Isa. 40, 65)
- Jesus' proclamation of the gospel of God (compare Mk. 1:14–15 with Isa. 40:9; 52:7; 61:1–2)

Mark signals the most profound connection between the promise of God's salvation in Isaiah and the gospel of Jesus Christ, which is none other than the gospel of God. As we saw in the previous chapter, this introduction to Mark's narrative thus identifies the arrival of Jesus as the advent of God's promised new exodus, the coming of God to liberate and restore Israel. In Jesus' coming, God has come. Jesus is God's agent of salvation who heralds the presence of God's dominion.

Mark 1:14–15 provides a programmatic summary of the message of Jesus: "The long-awaited time has been fulfilled; the kingdom of God has drawn near. Repent and believe the gospel!" On the one hand, Jesus' message is directed backward, so that it embraces the hopes of Israel for divine intervention in history to bring an end to exile and to restore peace and justice. On the other, this announcement points to the present in-breaking of the new reality in which God is king. Jesus' mission is thus intimately related to the inauguration of God's kingdom. What is more, according to Mark's synopsis of Jesus' proclamation, the new era initiated by Jesus' ministry has clear and present ramifications for life before God. People are to respond in the belief that God has come, embracing this new reality with their whole lives. The activity of God is prevenient: People are to respond *because* the ancient project of God has been initiated in Jesus' ministry—and not *in order that* God's work might be established.

That the message of Jesus can be summarized in terms of the kingdom of God points not only to the importance of the concept of the kingdom in his ministry but also to the presumption of some prior knowledge of the kingdom among Jesus' audience. This does not mean that Jesus' message is necessarily tied to popular definitions of the kingdom, but it does suggest that he could employ the phrase with confidence that his audiences would have shared with him some general understanding of its significance. Particularly with the rise of the prophets Amos and Hosea in the eighth century B.C.E., Israel turned its eyes to the future activity of God in history. For them, hope focused on the coming of the Lord in history as king. Later, Isaiah would describe the triumph of God as deliverer and sovereign in anticipation of the glorious reign of God (for example, Isa. 24:23; 30:33; 32:1; 33:17, 20–22). This portrait of God is not restricted to the prophets, however. The concept of God as king is present in the earliest history of the nation, as God serves as deliverer, leader, and law-giver in Israel's experience of exodus from Egypt and settlement in the land of promise. Not surprisingly, the language of kingship surfaces most clearly in the period of the monarchy; irrespective of what human king sat on Israel's throne, the true king was God, and it was God who then defined faithful kingship. Then, in the prophets, God's coming reign was announced as a symbol of Israel's renewal. In Isaiah's words, the good news is focused in this proclamation, "Your God reigns!" (Isa. 52:7).

How would Jesus' contemporaries have understood the kingdom of God? Among the list of possible features, three are essential. First, the kingdom of God entails the restoration of Israel, but is not limited to its national boundaries. God's kingdom is cosmic in its proportions, and so must address all the nations of the world. Second, the kingdom of God is nothing less than the coming of God to set things right. God's rule spells justice, the triumph of righteousness, and establishment of peace in the world, shalom. Third, the kingdom of God has to do with the coming *of God*. That is, anticipation of universal shalom was not necessarily tied to a messiah or messianic figure. To proclaim the arrival of the kingdom would be to announce the arrival of God to rule.

What is the relationship of these expectations to the ministry of Jesus? Do these hopes find their fulfillment in the coming of Jesus? The only possible answer is equivocal: yes *and* no. We must say yes because this is precisely what the gospels broadcast, that Jesus not only shared these expectations but actually regarded them as actualized in his ministry. Jesus both announces the kingdom and is its bearer. Wherever Jesus is engaged in ministry, there the kingdom of God is at hand—present in his work, active through him personally. At the same time, we must answer no because Jesus did not perform in the expected way, at least not in the way anticipated by those texts that proposed militaristic resolution. According to the gospels of Matthew and Luke, even John the Baptist was baffled by the direction of Jesus' mission: Where is the anticipated fiery judgment on Israel's enemies (Mt. 3:11–12; 11:2–3; Lk. 3:16–17; 7:18–20)?

If we follow the gospels, then, we realize that Jesus interpreted his mission from within the story of Israel, and specifically within the story of God's fidelity to the people. The time of restoration was at hand, evil was being rolled back, peace with justice was being established throughout the world, and God was present to rule—all in the ministry of Jesus, but not in ways commonly articulated among Jesus' contemporaries. For him, disclosure of the will of God meant standing at the threshold of fresh ways of conceiving God's work, and stepping across it. No longer working at cross-purposes with the ancient purpose of God, people find themselves in sync with God's own aims and active in God's redemptive project. The new exodus was under way, the new era was breaking in upon the old, and all of this was manifest in Jesus' person and work.

The Mission of Jesus

The question of Jesus' mission to save can be expanded further by exploring briefly three representative texts in which Jesus' aims are set out. The first derives from the gospel of Mark:

> Jesus went out again beside the sea; the whole crowd gathered around him, and he taught them. As he was walking along, he saw Levi son of Alphaeus sitting at the tax booth, and he said to him. "Follow me." And he got up and followed him.
>
> And as he sat down at dinner in Levi's house, many tax collectors and sinners were also sitting with Jesus and his disciples—for there were many who followed him. When the scribes of the Pharisees saw that he was eating with sinners and tax collectors, they said to his disciples, "Why does he eat with tax collectors and sinners?" When Jesus heard this, he said to them, "Those who are well have no need of a physician, but those who are sick; I have come to call not the righteous but sinners." (Mark 2:13–17)

In these two paragraphs, Jesus crosses social and religious boundaries to include in his circle of disciples and friends people at home at the periphery of acceptable society.

Our reading of this episode is enhanced if we grasp three aspects of Jesus' social world. The first is the importance of meals. What one ate and with whom had to do with the satiation of hunger, of course, but also signaled social and religious messages in ancient Judaism. Table fellowship had to do with intimacy; to share a meal with others involved including them as extended family, so to speak. For many Jews, therefore, and especially for Pharisees, the table was the focus of issues of clean and unclean, acceptable and unacceptable. Second, among the range of possible occupations in first-century Palestine, collecting tolls (or "taxes" in the NRSV) was one of the least reputable. Toll collectors were the entrepreneurs of Roman antiquity, but they paid a heavy price for the wealth they were able to accumulate. This is because, among the social elite, what mattered was "old money" or "landed wealth"; those, like toll collectors, who had to earn their wealth, had no place in society's upper echelons. In popular opinion among Jews and other Romans, moreover, toll collectors were regarded as snoops, small-brained, and social drivel. Third, "sinners" were not necessarily doers of great evil, nor were they simply people who failed to measure up to the requirements of the Jewish law. Rather, "sinner" had become in first-century Judaism a label to be placed on persons who failed to follow God in the way prescribed by one or another group within Judaism. That is, persons belonging to one Jewish group might refer to those of another group as "sinners," regarding them as little better than Gentiles.

Mark's portrait is especially stark, then, and it is little wonder that the legal experts question Jesus' behavior and attempt to influence his disciples to join them in censuring him. He has extended table intimacy to society's throwaways. In doing so, he interprets his behavior within a health care model: toll collectors and sinners are sick, he is a physician. Crossing boundaries between the well and the sick is precisely what physicians do, and this justifies Jesus' behavior. Jesus thus draws on biblical notions of the Lord as healer and of divine redemption as healing, where healing is defined as restoration to relationship with the Lord and the people—that is, as forgiveness.[10]

A second text, or group of texts, is drawn from Luke. Luke includes the episode of the calling of Levi and the banquet that follows (Lk. 5:27–32), but develops the importance of this presentation of

---

[10]See chapter 2.

Jesus even further by underscoring the hostility Jesus attracted on account of his table practices and partners at meal (for example, Lk. 14; 15:1–2), and by telling the story of Zacchaeus (Lk. 19:1–10), with its close parallels to the story of Levi.[11] Both reveal the low status of toll collectors, both associate toll collectors with the label "sinner," both indicate responses of discipleship (involving possessions and extending hospitality to Jesus), and both generalize from Jesus' encounter to summarize the nature of Jesus' mission: "I have come to call not the righteous but sinners to repentance" (Lk. 5:32) and, "For the Son of Man came to seek out and to save the lost" (19:10).

Zacchaeus is a strange character within the gospel of Luke. He is introduced to us as wealthy and as a ruler (or chief) among toll collectors, and this in a gospel narrative where the wealthy and rulers generally appear in opposition toward Jesus.[12] He is also a toll collector and is regarded by the crowd as a sinner, and this in a gospel where such persons habitually welcome Jesus and are welcomed by him.[13] By the end of the account, Jesus describes Zacchaeus as a "son of Abraham" (Lk. 19:9), a status that is evidenced in Zacchaeus' behavior with his money: He gives half of what he has to the poor and makes fourfold restitution to any who are cheated under his watch (cp. Lk. 3:10–14). Additionally, Jesus regards Zacchaeus as someone who has been "lost," but now restored. From Luke's account, it is obvious that Zacchaeus is looked upon within his own community as an outsider ("a sinner," Lk. 19:7), but Jesus restores him to full status among the people of God.

This is consistent with Jesus' mission and message throughout the gospel of Luke. In Luke 4:18–19, he announces that his mission is "to bring good news to the poor," a mission that is defined in three ways. First, it is a mission to "the poor"—who, in the gospel of Luke are identified above all as those who live at or beyond the frontiers of larger society. "Poor" is a large category of persons that includes the economically dispossessed, to be sure, but also those who are pushed to the margins of their own communities on account of gender, family

---

[11]On what follows, see Joel B. Green, "Good News to Whom? Jesus and the 'Poor' in the Gospel of Luke," in *Jesus of Nazareth: Lord and Christ: Essays on the Historical Jesus and New Testament Christology,* ed. Joel B. Green and Max Turner (Grand Rapids, Mich.: Wm. B. Eerdmans, 1995), 59–74 (69–74).

[12]See Lk. 1:51, 53; 6:24; 8:41, 49; 12:13–21; 13:14; 14:12–14; 16:19–31; 18:18–30.

[13]See Lk. 3:12; 5:27–32; 7:29; 15:1–2; 18:9–14.

heritage, disease, religious purity, ethnicity, and so on. Second, Jesus' mission is one of "release"—which, in the gospel of Luke, is developed in a variety of ways with regard to restoration to human wholeness—including socioeconomic relations, forgiveness, and liberty from the shackles of evil.[14] Third, in Jesus' sermon in Luke 4:16–30, he develops his mission in relation to the prophets Elijah and Elisha. Elijah, he points out, was sent by God to a woman, a non-Jew, a widow, while Elisha had been sent to a non-Jew whose disease, leprosy, symbolized his distance from Israel's God. (See Lev. 13—14.) With reference to these examples, Jesus emphasizes that "good news to the poor" embraces the widow, the unclean, the Gentile, and all others whom society regards as misfits and outcasts.

Taken together, these three statements of ministry (Lk. 4:16–30; 5:27–32; 19:1–10) point to Jesus' mission as opening the way for the inclusion of people in God's kingdom, for salvation, who otherwise have no apparent claim on God. They are the poor to whom Jesus proclaims "good news," and this is key to the identity of his messianic mission.

A final example derives from the gospel of John. Commenting on the exchange between Jesus and Nicodemus (see Jn. 3:1–21), the evangelist observes, "Indeed, God did not send the Son into the world to condemn the world, but in order that the world might be saved through him" (Jn. 3:17). The significance of this claim is set in relief by two observations—first, that it was customary in Jewish end-time hope that the coming of God's dominion would bring judgment on God's enemies; and, second, that this way of thinking presumed with reference to God's care a prodigious distance between Israel and Israel's enemies. John's commentary mitigates this emphasis on judgment in two ways. On the one hand, salvation is not for Israel only but for "the world." As John 3:16 has it, the love of God and so the saving mission of Jesus are oriented to the world, extending beyond boundaries drawn by race or culture or nation. Second, the coming of salvation does not preclude the possibility of belief, but actually invites and, indeed, enables belief. The advent of Jesus does not mark

---

[14]Cf. Lk. 1:77; 3:3; 5:20–21, 23–24; 7:47–49; 11:4; 12:10; 13:10–17; 17:3–4; 23:34; 24:47; Joel B. Green, *The Theology of the Gospel of Luke,* New Testament Theology (Cambridge: Cambridge Univ. Press, 1995), 78–79, 113–17.

the pronouncement of the final verdict, but rather occasions further opportunity for positive response.

As John 3:1–15 makes clear, provision of further opportunity is important, since (1) the condition for entering life with God is belief and (2) the response of faith is not available to darkened minds and hearts apart from divine intervention. Nicodemus, a Pharisee and legal expert, who represents the Jewish elite, is a case in point. In spite of his status and expertise in handling Torah, he seems incapable of understanding the message of Jesus. A complete reversal is needed— what we have called a conversion of the imagination is required; for Jesus, this entails "being born from above." Nicodemus' failure to grasp Jesus' words illustrates his present alienation from the thought patterns of God. Jesus' response to Nicodemus is therefore plastered with irony: "Are you a teacher of Israel, and yet you do not understand these things?" (Jn. 3:10).

The good news is that it is precisely to effect this reversal, to enable this belief, that Jesus has come, and this belief is available in the very presence of doubt (Jn. 20:19–29). From the perspective of John, his own narrative of Jesus' wondrous signs can serve to bring persons into a faith-full encounter with the Messiah. (See Jn. 20:30– 31.) Using Exodus imagery, John draws again the analogy from Israel of old to new exodus, so as to declare the basis of human salvation: "And just as Moses lifted up the serpent in the wilderness, so must the Son of Man be lifted up, that whoever believes in him may have eternal life" (Jn. 3:14–15). The "lifting up" of Jesus refers in the gospel of John to his suffering and death on the cross.[15] Just as gazing at the serpent was God's provision for restored health in Numbers 21, so Jesus, in his suffering and death, embodies God's will to give eternal life. (See Jn. 14:1–11.)

The Atoning Death of Jesus

A further mission statement that occupies a prominent place in the gospels of Matthew and Mark reports Jesus' words, "The Son of Man came not to be served but to serve, and to give his life a ransom for many" (Mt. 20:28; Mk. 10:45). This text functions both to confirm the other-oriented ethic Jesus proposed in his ministry and to provide Jesus'

---

[15]Cf. Jn. 8:28; 12:32–33; 18:32.

self-disclosure of the life goal given him by God. "Ransom" invites potential reflection on two images. One is borrowed from the Roman slave trade, where a ransom might serve as the price of emancipation, after which the one freed belonged to the one who paid the price; in terms of understanding the efficacy of Jesus' death, this image is of questionable value since we find no suggestion here that, in Jesus' crucifixion, God (or Jesus) "paid" anyone or anything to win our liberation. The second is of greater importance, and derives from Israel's own past: God "ransomed" Israel, delivering the people from slavery in Egypt (Ex. 6:6; 16:13). Jesus both instructs his followers to devote their lives to the service of others and reveals at the same time the purpose of his own, even to the point that he will embrace death on behalf of others. In this way, Mark shows that Jesus' death effects the liberation inherent in new exodus hope at the same time that it calls upon Jesus' followers to incarnate an ethic of service to others.[16]

Widening our perspective in relation to other writers in the New Testament, we encounter an extensive menu of ways to understand Jesus' death. This is because of both the necessity to articulate the significance of the cross in relation to particular needs in the mission and in Christian communities, and the fact that the death of Jesus is an event of such pivotal importance to the plan of God that its importance cannot be measured.[17] The New Testament writers seem never to tire of generating new models for communicating the saving importance of the cross. Taken as a whole, however, these images congregate around five spheres of Roman public life: the court of law (for example, justification), the world of commerce (for example, redemption), personal relationships (for example, reconciliation), worship (for example, sacrifice), and the battleground (for example, triumph over evil). This variety might appropriately lead us to the conclusion that the significance of Jesus' death could not be represented without remainder by any one concept, theory, or metaphor. Paul himself can write of substitution, representation, sacrifice, justification,

---

[16]Importantly, the scene Mark records in Mk. 14:3–9 evidences the correlation of sacrificial service—in this case, the woman's generous act in preparing Jesus for burial—with recognition of the centrality of Jesus' impending death to his mission.

[17]See John Driver, *Understanding the Atonement for the Mission of the Church* (Scottdale, Pa.,: Herald, 1986); Mark D. Baker and Joel B. Green, *Recovering the Scandal of the Cross: Atonement in New Testament and Contemporary Contexts* (Downers Grove, Ill.: InterVarsity, 2000).

forgiveness, reconciliation, triumph over the powers, redemption, and more. For Hebrews, on the other hand, the notion of sacrifice is paramount, with Jesus presented as both the perfect high priest and the perfect sacrificial victim. First Peter speaks of Jesus' death as a ransom and sacrifice, while Revelation presents Jesus' death in terms of military triumph and redemption. And this is only the beginning.

It may be helpful to highlight one further text, Romans 5:1–11, wherein we find that the death of Christ is the ultimate expression of the love of God: "But God demonstrates his love for us in that while we were still sinners Christ died for us." (Rom. 5:8, author's translation). Paul's message here highlights four important points. First, the love of God for humanity is immeasurable, for there are no human parallels by which to comprehend it. Second, God's love is prevenient; it precedes and is not dependent on human activity or response. Third, Paul's audience can be certain that their suffering has significance because the suffering of Christ has proven so meaningful. Through his death we have been justified, saved, and reconciled. In the midst of our impotence, Christ took on the measure of our powerlessness and died in our place. As a result of his death, we share in his life, and we find that our own suffering has significance in relation to his. Fourth, we are told that *God* demonstrates love by means of what *Christ* did. We might have anticipated that God's love would be revealed in God's own deed, and this would certainly have been the case were Paul sketching an atonement theology oriented toward divine recrimination. Paul's way of putting things shows instead the oneness of the purpose and activity of God and God's Son in the cross.

As the apostle puts it elsewhere, "in Christ God was reconciling the world to himself" (2 Cor. 5:19). In another passage where descriptive terms for the saving effects of Jesus' death congregate (2 Cor. 5:14—6:12: *substitution, representation, sacrifice, justification, forgiveness,* and *new creation*), Paul carefully shows how the work of God and of Christ are one. What is more, Paul does not speak of any need for mutual reconciliation. "The world" is estranged from God and needs to be brought back into relationship with God, but God is not estranged from "the world." For this reason, Paul has no need to show how God can be appeased, or how God might come to extend love again. Rather, Paul affirms that God's love always has the upper hand in divine-human relations, and that the work of Christ had as its effect the bringing of "the world" back to God.

What Must I Do to Be Saved?

How are humans to respond to God's drawing near to save? In order to gain our bearings around this question, we can examine the account of the encounter of Paul and Silas with the Philippian jailer and his family in Acts 16:23–40. Upon Paul and Silas' miraculous release from prison by an earthquake, the jailor gives voice to our question, "Sirs, what must I do to be saved?" (Acts 16:30).

The introduction of the jailer is abrupt. Told to confine Paul and Silas securely (Acts 16:23), he imprisoned them "in the innermost cell and fastened their feet in stocks" (Acts 16:24), as though they were "dangerous low class felons."[18] Thinking that those under his charge have escaped in the aftermath of the earthquake, he apparently fears his own death (cp. Acts 12:18–19) and opts for the honor of suicide over the shame of execution (Acts 16:27). How should we read his question to Paul and Silas? The problem revolves around the first word—in Greek, *kyrioi*, translated by the NRSV as "sirs," but usually translated "lords." In spite of parallel questions in Luke 3:10–14 and Acts 2:37, it is doubtful that we should hear in his voice a request for salvation in the full, Christian sense as this is developed in the Lukan narrative. Neither should we follow the NRSV, however, in suggestion that the jailer's address to Paul and Silas as *kyrioi* is an attempt at polite address; note that, only hours ago these men were humiliated, beaten prisoners, not persons of respect. Rather, the jailer has had to reconsider his evaluation of them on account of the incredible character of their escape. Either he fears them, as though they were more than human, or he sees in them a power capable of rescuing him from his certain fate in the service of the emperor. Thus, he addresses them with a term, "lords," prominently used in the imperial cult of the emperor. The message he receives, which Luke characterizes as "the word of *the Lord*" (Acts 16:32), names Jesus as *Lord* (Acts 16:31). That is, Paul and Silas deflect the honor given them by the jailer and call attention instead to Jesus. They name in an unambiguous fashion the source both of the power behind these spectacular events and of authentic deliverance.

The effect is that an enemy—who because of his own oppressed status must fear for his life even though he has made a livelihood as

---

[18]Brian Rapske, *The Book of Acts and Paul in Roman Custody*, The Book of Acts in Its First Century Setting, vol. 3 (Grand Rapids, Mich.: Wm. B. Eerdmans, 1994), 126–27.

the instrument of oppression for others—and with him his whole household, are transformed. Paul and Silas call upon the jailer and his household to "believe on the Lord Jesus" (Acts 16:31). Their response is full-orbed: They believe, rejoice, extend hospitality to Paul and Silas, and are baptized. The true Lord is named, such that this household comes under the lordship of Jesus rather than that of Caesar.[19] We would like to know the rest of the story perhaps—for example, what shape "repentance" might take in the everyday life of this jailer (see Luke 3:10–14)—but this is not the narrative Luke has provided. The focus falls rather on the validation of the faith and accompanying practices of this jailer and his household. Baptism in this case thus signifies God's acceptance of these persons, authenticates their faith and hospitable practices as markers of the new order over which Jesus is Lord, and signals the ongoing progress of the Christian mission.

This account is instructive for us for at least two reasons. First, it illustrates, even in Acts, that there is no one way of describing the appropriate response to the gospel; and, second, it exposes the dichotomy we sometimes place between "faith" and "life" as a false one.

What of the variety of responses to the good news? True, throughout Acts, the call for a radically different understanding of the world calls for response, but the narrative presents different ways of construing conversion. In Acts 26:17–18, Paul recounts his commission from Jesus, who sends him "to open their eyes so that they might turn from darkness to light and from the power of Satan to God." In this case, Luke draws on the familiar language of religious conversion, but interprets it so as to situate the redemptive purpose of God within the cosmic battle, one kingdom giving way to the other. Elsewhere the Christian mission can be represented as one of debate and dialogue—a battle of interpretation, as it were (for example, Acts 13:16, 38, 41; 17:3; 19:8–10). Among Greek audiences, Paul calls for people to leave the way of idolatry and turn to "the living God" (Acts 14:15–16). Although Luke is concerned with conversion from one form of life to another, then, he outlines no "typical" way of understanding (and no technology of) conversion. The "order of salvation" that runs through these accounts is this: God initiates, people

---

[19]The jailer's offer of hospitality is itself an illegal act, according to Rapske (*Paul in Roman Custody*, 390–92), and this underscores the shift in his allegiances.

hear the message of salvation, people respond. In fact, this is the heart of Peter's defense of the inclusion of Gentiles in the community of God's people in 15:7–11: "God made a choice"; "Gentiles...hear the message of the good news"; they become "believers."

To deny that Luke presents a technology of response is not to deny the possibility of some generalizations, however. (1) *Baptism in the name of Jesus* is a normal response, as suggested by the Ethiopian's question, "Look, here is water! What is to prevent me from being baptized?" (Acts 8:36; cf. 2:41; 8:12; 9:18; 10:47–48; 16:15; et al.). Within the Lukan narrative, *baptism* takes its meaning in part from the ministry of John (Lk. 3:1–20), with the result that it expresses a desire to embrace God's purpose anew and to be embraced into the community of those similarly oriented around the way of God. (2) *Repentance* (or "turning to God") is often mentioned explicitly as an appropriate response to God's salvific work (cf. Acts 2:38; 3:19; 5:31; 11:18; 17:30; 20:21; 26:20). Again, Luke's portrayal of this response is rooted in his account of the ministry of John (esp. Lk. 3:1–14), where repentance is marked by behavior that grows out of and demonstrates the fact that one has indeed committed oneself to service in God's purpose (cf. Lk. 3:10–14; Acts 26:20). (3) That Christians are sometimes called "believers" signals the importance of *faith* in Luke's understanding of salvation (cf. Acts 2:44; 3:16; 11:17; 13:39; 14:9; 15:7; 16:30–31; 18:8).

Let me turn now to the second issue—that is, the false distinction between "faith" and "life" with regard to human response to the gift of salvation. Here I refer to a variety of dualisms by which we have learned to make sense of our lives: my inner self versus my outer self, my "being" versus my "doing," right faith versus right actions, and the like. It is imperative that we recognize the degree to which this way of constructing our lives has been culturally determined, and the degree to which it runs counter to the witness of scripture. As we noted in chapter 1, Charles Taylor observes how personal identity has come to be shaped by such assumptions such as these: Human dignity lies in self-sufficiency and self-determination; identity is grasped in self-referential terms: I am who I am; persons have an inner self, which is the authentic self; and basic to authentic personhood are self-autonomy and self-legislation. Biblical anthropology, on the other hand, places a premium on the construction of the self as deeply embedded in social relationships, a premium on the integrity of the community and thus the contribution of individuals to that integrity, and a premium on the assumption that a person *is* one's behavior— that is, that one's dispositions are on display in one's practices. To take seriously the implications of this change in perspective for our present interests, this would mean that transformation in the arena of one's essential beliefs, commitments, and allegiances is unavoidably on display in one's behavior and practices in the world. Conversion, then, is the transformation of our imaginations, which is necessarily rooted and manifest in faith and life. Put simply, the call to salvation is the call to live according to another world order; faith is entrusting ourselves to God's view of things (even when the evidence before us seems contrary); and this faith is on display in faithfulness.

Seen from this vantage point, conversion entails *autobiographical reconstruction*. As Peter Berger and Thomas Luckmann put it, "Everything preceding the alteration is now apprehended as leading toward it…, everything following it as flowing from its new reality. This involves a reinterpretation of past biography *in toto*, following the formula 'Then I *thought*…now I *know*.'"[20] Conversion shatters one's past and reassembles it in accordance with the new life of the converted; former understandings of oneself and one's experiences are regarded as erroneous and are provided new meaning (cf. Luke 9:23). "From now on, therefore," Paul writes, "we regard no one from a human point of view; even though we once knew Christ from a human point of view, we know him no longer in that way. So if anyone is in Christ, there is a new creation: everything old has passed away; see, everything has become new!" (2 Cor. 5:16–17).

More pervasive in the New Testament are those instances where one's reshaped allegiances and dispositions are expressed in terms that reflect a fresh grasp of God's character as well as fresh conceptualizations of the nature of God's people. This generally comes through understanding one's place within the history of God's purpose, or writing oneself into the ancient story of God's work with Abraham and Sarah, Moses, and Ruth. Stephen and Paul, for example, prove themselves to be masterful narrators of the history of Israel (for example, Acts 7; 13:16–41). For Paul, of course, this comes after his own extensive formation in the scriptures of Israel (see Acts 22:3) has

---

[20]Peter L. Berger and Thomas Luckmann, *The Social Construction of Reality: A Treatise in the Sociology of Knowledge* (New York: Doubleday, 1966), 160.

been recast through his encounter with Jesus as the Risen Lord (Acts 9:1–19). The whole of Israel's history and self-understanding is now reevaluated for presentation in light of the newly found understanding of God's purpose resident in Jesus' crucifixion and exaltation. Conversion is thus the process of *embracing a life-world*, a conversion of the imagination, on display in the Christian community.

Interestingly, this new life-world comes to expression most fully in the context of one of the characteristic practices of the Christian community. This is prayer, which provides the opportunity for the disclosure of God's salvific purpose especially at pivotal points in the mission. The book of Acts portrays prayer as a community-defining practice that invariably leads to the expansion of the community. This is because the habits of prayer counseled by Jesus serve as an ongoing catalyst for the conformation of the community around the unlimited mercy of God (cf. Lk. 6:35–36; 11:1–13). Prayer of this sort allows for the infusion of a worldview centered on the gracious God, on dependence on God, on the imitation of God, and on the disclosure of God's purpose for humanity, all understood against an eschatological horizon in which the coming of God in sovereignty and redemption figures prominently.

With the identification of prayer as a community-defining practice, I have already drawn attention to the importance of viewing conversion as *incorporation into a new community*, including adopting the rituals and behaviors peculiar to or definitive of that new community. In the Lukan narrative, this is evident immediately in Acts 2:42–47. The generalizations about the community of Jesus' followers sketched here amplify the response urged by Peter in Acts 2:38, "Repent, and be baptized." Baptism functions, on the one hand, as the medium by which repentance comes to expression and, on the other, as the sign that forgiveness has been granted.[21] To put it differently, baptism serves a community-defining role— communicating on the part of the baptized an unswerving loyalty to the Lord and on the part of the church the full incorporation of the baptized into the community. Baptism is both response and gift. What is more, baptism in Acts has as its consequence, among other things, economic sharing (for example, 2:41–47) and the extension of

---

[21]See Lars Hartman, *'Into the Name of the Lord Jesus': Baptism in the Early Church*, Studies of the New Testament in Its World (Edinburgh: T. & T. Clark, 1997), 130.

hospitality (for example, Acts 10:47–48; 16:14–15, 28–34)—behaviors, then, that must be included under the heading of "fruits worthy of repentance" (Lk. 3:7–14).

Epilogue

We can get at the issues addressed in this chapter by phrasing the question this way: What does it mean "to perform" salvation? God is actualizing God's purpose to save, and in doing so, throughout Israel's history, has set out ways in which blessings might be mediated to the people. Chief among these blessings is the gift of relationship, and particularly restored relationship, with God, out of which unfolds the way of life for which we were created. God acts out, or performs, God's will, and the consequence is that the way of salvation is opened to us. Importantly, this "us" knows no boundaries, but includes all who are willing to embrace and act on the grace of seeing what could not otherwise be seen, to stand at the threshold of fresh ways of conceiving God's work and step across.

The "performance" of salvation requires more than one actor, however. If God's is the aim we are to serve, it is nonetheless true that God's drawing near to save forces a crisis among people. A decision is necessary: to oppose or to serve that purpose. This is precisely the juncture in the road that the advent of Jesus represents. Of course, the coming of Jesus opens the way of salvation and enables faith. His ministry, death, and resurrection signal the expression of the gospel of God in the most pristine sense. With the self-disclosure of God in Jesus Christ, the way is open, but it is a way that must be taken. The community of the saved are those who elect no longer to work at cross-purposes with God, and who thus find themselves in sync with God's own aims and active in God's redemptive project. Faith and faithfulness cannot be distinguished in the lives of those so thoroughly converted. Those who perceive God in Christ ultimately revealing himself in the world must behave in that world as new persons. This is because they are, indeed, new persons, whose allegiances are given over to the reality breaking into the world.[22]

---

[22]Bruce Chilton and J. I. H. McDonald, *Jesus and the Ethics of the Kingdom* (Grand Rapids, Mich.: Wm. B. Eerdmans, 1987), 110–34.

5

THE COMMUNITY OF SALVATION:
THEN, NOW, AND THE FUTURE

The Bible tells a grand story. It is true that, within its pages, we find numerous side stories, episodes that seem to take us along strange paths or corridors not easily integrated into the whole. For this reason, each reading of scripture invites a different emphasis, since each reading allows one or another motif to become more prominent than in the last. The canon of scripture places limits on the variety of "tellings" that the Bible can support, however. Thus far we have named two primary points in the grand narrative of scripture that provide unavoidable structure and shape to the whole. It is simply inconceivable that we could plot the biblical narrative without reference to the beginning of the narrative and its middle—that is, to the purpose and action of God in creation (beginning) and redemption (middle). Moreover, a commitment to the whole of scripture makes necessary that we comprehend this "middle" in two movements: the liberating work of God in exodus and the saving work of God in the advent of Jesus Christ. That is, if we take seriously the definition given the story of God's purpose (its origins in God's own character and its actualization in human history), there is no bypassing Israel or Jesus.[1] Since Aristotle, though, a narrative has been characterized as possessing not only a beginning and middle, but also an end. In this chapter, we turn, finally, to the climax toward which the biblical story is heading. This is the end that, because it is already revealed to us in its essentials, casts its shadow backward and determines how we trace the flow of the narrative of God's project today. And, if we find our homes in that narrative, it back-shadows the character of our hopes and lives and pulls us forward into its vision of the way things ought to be.

Our aim in this concluding chapter, then, is two-fold—first, to set out a vision of where this story is heading. In classic terms, this is eschatology, our understanding of the last things. In the present case, our agenda is circumscribed by our primary interest in the biblical witness to salvation. What will it mean, in the end, to be saved? What we will discover is that end-time thinking, if it is genuinely to be biblical, cannot be lost in speculation or shallow optimism; rather, it must be fully integrated into our contemporary existence and sense of vocation. If we know where we are going—indeed, if we are committed to a particular destination—we can and ought to orient our lives fully around that destination. Second, then, we will explore how end-time thinking is for us intertwined with our understanding and experience of, and commitment to, the church. What is the nature of this salvation, which must be understood always as a process moving toward an end just beyond the horizon? What of the community, the church, in which salvation is embodied and lived and sought? What is its character and mission? Not surprisingly, questions such as these are interwoven with many others, about the nature of Christ, for example, or the work of the Holy Spirit, with the result that our exploration will involve us in interaction with a variety of motifs.

The End of Salvation

The message of scripture is clear: This is not all there is. The importance of this affirmation is evident already in accounts of Jesus' interaction with his detractors. He announced the coming of God to

[1]This emphasis on Israel has often been overlooked in Christian theology, but there are important signs of recovery, together with a renewal of interest in the place of the Old Testament as Christian scripture—cf., e.g., R. Kendall Soulen, *The God of Israel and Christian Theology* (Minneapolis: Fortress Press, 1996); Ronald E. Diprose, *Israel in the Development of Christian Thought* (Rome: Istituto Biblico Evangelico Italiano, 2000); Christopher R. Seitz, *Word without End: The Old Testament as Abiding Theological Witness* (Grand Rapids, Mich.: Wm. B. Eerdmans, 1998).

save, yet Rome still exercised its power and human tragedy still occurred daily. As Luke records, people in Jesus' day might speak of "the Galileans whose blood Pilate had mingled with their sacrifices," or those eighteen persons "who were killed when the tower of Siloam fell on them" (Lk. 13:1–4). How do such occurrences square with "good news"? Jesus response was twofold. First, he pressed his audience to see what could not be seen with eyes unaided by faith. The gospels' witness to Jesus' extending recovery of sight to the blind (for example, Lk. 7:21–22; Jn. 9) is as much about illumination as it is about ophthalmology. As Elisha once prayed regarding his fearful servant, "O LORD...open his eyes that he may see" those divine resources arrayed against the enemy (2 Kings 6:1–17), so Jesus pressed for and enabled people to expand their imaginations in order to account for the sometimes less obvious and overshadowed work of God among them. Second, Jesus assured his listeners that the in-breaking of God's dominion was a process, that God's work as yet remained unfinished, and that God would intervene to consummate this saving design.

These two emphases can be illustrated with reference to Jesus' story of a wealthy householder and his invitation list (Lk. 14:15–24), a story that is susceptible to two quite different readings.

> One of the dinner guests, on hearing this, said to him, "Blessed is anyone who will eat bread in the kingdom of God!" Then Jesus said to him, "Someone gave a great dinner and invited many. At the time for the dinner he sent his slave to say to those who had been invited, 'Come; for everything is ready now.' But they all alike began to make excuses. The first said to him, 'I have bought a piece of land, and I must go out and see it; please accept my regrets.' Another said, 'I have bought five yoke of oxen, and I am going to try them out; please accept my regrets.' Another said, 'I have just been married, and therefore I cannot come.' So the slave returned and reported this to his master. Then the owner of the house became angry and said to his slave, 'Go out at once into the streets and lanes of the town and bring in the poor, the crippled, the blind, and the lame.' And the slave said, 'Sir, what you ordered has been done, and there is still room.' Then the master said to the slave, 'Go out into the roads and lanes, and compel people to come in, so that my house may be filled. For I tell you, none of those who were invited will taste my dinner.'"

The first, and the more well-known, interpretation has it that this is a parable of the end-time banquet. In this case, the master of the house is God, who would have extended invitations to some who refused to attend, leading to extending the invitation further to include others, especially the marginalized and the Gentile. Typically, recipients of the first invitation are regarded as the Jews, or perhaps the Jewish leadership, whose relationship to the master is marred by the silly excuses given to explain their refusal to take their places at the banquet table. According to this reading, this is a parable of warning and of hope—hope to those on the periphery of acceptable society that they, too, will be included on the end-time invitation list; warning to those already on that list, lest they refuse to ready themselves and to accept the places reserved for them at the table.

An alternative reading would more firmly locate this story within its wider context in Luke 14, where Jesus has just instructed his table companions regarding their own table practices. In this instance, the question, Who will enjoy God's hospitality at the end-time banquet? is answered with reference to a second: Who is now enjoying the hospitality of your table? That is, one's place at the kingdom feast is determined by one's behavior in the present, with regard to the poor and dispossessed. Jesus counsels, "When you give a banquet, invite the poor, the crippled, the lame, and the blind. And you will be blessed, because they cannot repay you, for you will be repaid at the resurrection of the righteous" (Lk. 14:13–14). Now the central message is this: Will Jesus' audience include the outcast among their table intimates, without concern for payback and self-aggrandizement? According to this reading of the Lukan story, Jesus provides an exemplar of someone, a wealthy householder, who heard his message well, and put it into practice.

What holds these two interpretations together is the one exclamation of the anonymous guest, "Blessed is anyone who will eat bread in the kingdom of God!" One reading has it that Jesus responds by underscoring the character of this end-time banquet. The other has Jesus working, again, to reorient the way people see the present, and especially to embrace and embody the transformed dispositions that accompany God's present work in the world.[2]

---

[2]For details and further bibliography, see Joel B. Green, *The Gospel of Luke,* New International Commentary on the New Testament (Grand Rapids, Mich.: Wm. B. Eerdmans, 1997), 554–63.

Broadening our vision, we may observe the variety of, and often fantastic, ways in which the end is portrayed in the Bible. In an essay with the rather foreboding title, "Scientific Accounts of Ultimate Catastrophes in Our Life-Bearing Universe," William Stoeger speaks matter-of-factly about the certainty of the ultimate demise of life on this planet and, indeed, of the universe. Speaking only of our own world, he discusses the possibilities of destruction through impact with a massive asteroid or comet, the eventual decline and death of our sun, and the explosion of a supernova in a neighboring system. With reference to the cosmos as a whole, he discusses the eventuality that the universe will gradually fade or perhaps collapse in upon itself.[3] The biblical writers speak to something of the same eventualities, but with more surreal language, drawing on the imagination to portray coming realities that can scarcely be imagined.[4] For them, the language of choice is apocalyptic, the language of word-pictures, often fantastic.

The emergence of the shocking images we find in selected biblical writings—Daniel and Revelation, most prominently, but also Zechariah, Joel, Mark, and others—was due to the environment within which apocalyptic was born and nurtured. Apocalyptic was grounded in the social experience of powerlessness, marginalization, and the conviction that Israel's destiny would never be fulfilled within this world but would come in the next, as a consequence of God's direct intervention. As Paul Hanson puts it, "The ancient Jewish apocalyptic writings grew out of the courage to stare into the abyss on the edge of which an entire civilization tottered, and a willingness to describe what the fantasy of faith enabled the human eye to glimpse beyond tragedy."[5] The ambiguities of present history would make sense when portrayed on the greater mural of God's dealings in history and beyond history, on the earth and in the world of the supernatural.

Apocalyptic images of the future in the Bible congregate around a relatively stable series of motifs: (1) the immediacy of the end,

[3]William R. Stoeger, "Scientific Accounts of Ultimate Catastrophes in Our Life-Bearing Universe," in *The End of the World and the Ends of God: Science and Theology on Eschatology*, ed. John Polkinghorne and Michael Welker (Harrisburg, Pa.: Trinity, 2000), 19–28.

[4]This is an understatement of the present tension between theological and scientific narratives of the end. For orientation, see Polkinghorne and Welker, eds., *The End of the World and the Ends of God*.

[5]Paul D. Hanson, "Introduction," in *Visionaries and Their Apocalypses*, ed. Paul D. Hanson (London: SPCK; Philadelphia: Fortress, 1983), 1–15 (3).

(2) the cataclysmic character of the end, (3) the transformation of the cosmos, and (4) divine provision in the new era of salvation; and these grow out of two pervasive affirmations, concerning (5) the malignant ubiquity of evil and (6) the sovereign triumph of God.

(1) The Immediacy of the End: In the New Testament, the immediacy of the end is conveyed in a variety of images, including the thief who comes in the night (for example, Mt. 24:43; 1 Thess. 5:2, 4; 2 Pet. 3:10; Rev. 16:15), the master who returns after a long journey (Mk. 13:34–36; Lk. 12:35–38, 42–48), and the bridegroom who arrives in the middle of the night (Mt. 25:1–13). Additionally, lists of events or historical records could serve this purpose. In Daniel, for example, as in Revelation, many of the events that were to have happened before the end had already occurred when the book was first written. Similarly, in Mark 13, the events that would precede the end are plainly characteristic of most every age. These "signs of the times" insinuate strongly that the end is (always) imminent. "Immediacy" is not always in scripture a reference to "soon," however. Sometimes the New Testament writers want to urge the view that "the end is soon," but often they underscore instead the sense that "the end could come at any time, unexpectedly."

(2) The Cataclysmic Character of the End: Most apocalyptic texts that warn of the end of the world do so with reference to a stereotyped list of catastrophes expected to precede the final judgment. These include famine, earthquakes, wars, betrayal, signs in the heavens, and so on (for example, Joel 2; Mk. 13; Revelation). The apocalyptic discourse in Mark 13 also speaks of the destruction of the Jerusalem temple as a sign of the end, due no doubt to the centrality of the temple in defining the world of the Jewish people. Some writings also speak of the coming of a time of great tribulation (for example, Dan. 12:1; Mk. 13:24; Rev. 7:14), an unprecedented time of affliction numbered among the many woes that accompany the end. Second Peter 3:10 summarizes this idea: "The heavens will pass away with a loud noise, and the elements will be dissolved with fire." Importantly, these texts do more than describe the coming horror, but also put it in perspective. Perhaps most importantly, trials and tribulations are interpreted as "woes" that accompany the birth of the kingdom of God. Repeatedly, the suffering of the faithful is folded into the work of the Messiah, by which the redemptive work of God is brought to

consummation. Paul puts it this way: "I am now rejoicing in my sufferings for your sake, and in my flesh I am completing what is lacking in Christ's afflictions for the sake of his body, that is, the church" (Col. 1:24).[6] As such, they are defined as both necessary (and therefore not without significance in the divine plan) and temporary.

(3) The Transformation of the Cosmos: Second Peter also summarizes well the apocalyptic vision of reversal at the end: "we wait for new heavens and a new earth, where righteousness is at home" (3:13). John uses similar symbolism (Rev. 21), drawing explicit attention to the absence of death, mourning, crying, and pain, "for the old order has passed away" (Rev. 21:4, author's translation; compare, for example, Isa. 33:24; 65:20). Nor, John adds, will the new earth include any "sea"—a reference to the final triumph over evil, symbolized by the powers of chaos represented in the sea and the sea monster: the dragon (Job 7:12; Ps. 74:13), Leviathan (Job 40:15–24; Pss. 74:13–14; 104:26; Isa. 27:1); Rahab (Job 9:13; Ps. 89:10; Isa. 51:9–11), and the serpent (Job 26:13; Isa. 27:1).

Paul uses apocalyptic imagery to denote the transformation already overtaking creation "in Christ," when he remarks, "If anyone is in Christ, there is a new creation" (2 Cor. 5:17). Elsewhere, he observes that "the creation waits with eager longing for the revealing of the children of God; for the creation was subjected to futility, not of its own will but by the will of the one who subjected it, in hope that the creation itself will be set free from its bondage to decay and will obtain the freedom of the glory of the children of God" (Rom. 8:19–21). A more serious counter to the human tendency to regard ourselves as our own creators, apart from God, or to regard ourselves and our destinies apart from the whole of creation, could hardly be articulated. The final "revealing" (that is, "the end-time unveiling of God's salvation") locates a restored humanity within a restored cosmos. Mark's account of Jesus' wilderness temptations points in the same direction. That, in the wilderness, Jesus was "with the wild beasts" (Mk. 1:13) prefigures the end-time reversal of the distortion of the relationship between humanity and the animal world. Peaceful, harmonious relations, characteristic of life in Eden but contorted by

---

[6]Cf. John S. Pobee, *Persecution and Martyrdom in the Theology of Paul,* Journal for the Study of the New Testament Supplement Series 6 (Sheffield: JSOT Press, 1985).

human sin, are restored in the kingdom of God, introduced in the advent of Jesus.[7]

(4) Divine Provision in the New Era of Salvation: The apocalyptic vision is not all one of doom and gloom. It is true that apocalyptic writers express little hope in the recovery of the world in its present form, but this does not keep them from believing that God will bring "times of refreshing" (Acts 3:20) or that God is working in the present world to bring God's purposes to completion. God will provide for the people, though the shape of that provision is often context-specific. To people experiencing economic oppression or deprivation, God's provision might take the form of streets of gold (Revelation). To the hungry or to those who long for restored fellowship with God, the heavenly feast, provided and hosted by God, is an apt symbol of restoration (for example, Isa. 25:6; Lk. 14:15; Rev. 19:9).

(5) The Malignant Ubiquity of Evil: One of the primary concerns to which apocalyptic addresses itself is the problem of suffering in the world, particularly the suffering of the righteous. A crucial answer is provided in heightened emphasis on the authority of the devil and the demonic world, whose power is aligned against the aims of God and the lives of God's people. For these visionaries, evil could not be reduced to an individual's bad choices, but was a cosmic reality. This does not mean that evil can simply be personified in the devil, however; especially in Daniel and the book of Revelation, evil is embodied in social structures, political entities, and governmental institutions, and is all-pervasive. Evil must be taken seriously. So powerful and widespread is evil that it would not disappear or be overcome by merely human effort, however loving and good. Divine intervention would be needed, and it is precisely this intervention that is promised.

(6) The Sovereign Triumph of God: As we have noted, end-time images are often accompanied by end-time timetables. These timetables are not easily converted into dates on our calendars, and this has frustrated those who are fascinated with interpreting "the signs of the times" in order to fix the date of the end of the world. But this is not their purpose. Rather, apocalyptic lists of events that must

---

[7]Cf. Job 5:22–23; Isa. 11:6–9; 65:25; and, more fully, Richard Bauckham, "Jesus and the Wild Animals (Mark 1:13): A Christological Image for an Ecological Age," in *Jesus of Nazareth: Lord and Christ: Essays on the Historical Jesus and New Testament Christology,* ed. Joel B. Green and Max Turner (Grand Rapids, Mich.: Wm. B. Eerdmans, 1995), 3–21.

happen in preparation for the end serve, first, to indicate that the suffering and woe that accompany these days comprise no surprise to God. The God of Israel knew of them beforehand, and has incorporated them into the means by which to bring final restoration. Second, then, they serve to remind us that, despite appearances to the contrary, God is in control.

The book of Revelation underscores these two points in profound ways. Revelation begins and ends with God's self-declaration, "I am the Alpha and the Omega" (Rev. 1:8; 21:6; compare 1:17; 22:13)— using the first and last letters of the Greek alphabet to affirm God's status as the beginning and the end, the first and the last, the One who was, is, and is to come (Rev. 1:4, 8; 4:8; 11:17; 16:5). Moreover, the single most pervasive portrait of God in Revelation is the One who sits on the true throne. The word itself, *throne*, appears more than forty times in the book, almost always of God in glory and sovereignty; glory and power belong to the One on the throne; God is the sovereign actor who brings history to its predetermined end, who brings salvation, who pronounces judgment, who makes all things new.[8] Satan's power is false, a carbon copy of genuine authority, and his throne will be crushed. God will be God when current turmoil has ended, for God is the one who will bring the end.

The Future Is for the Present

For what purpose are all of these words concerning the future, the end? In some instances in scripture, end-time talk provides warnings and promises that should serve as motivation for the present. One New Testament writer seems to have this in mind when he writes, "But, in accordance with his promise, we wait for new heavens and a new earth, where righteousness is at home. Therefore, beloved, while you are waiting for these things, strive to be found by him at peace, without spot or blemish" (2 Pet. 3:13–14; see 3:1–18). Threats of hell or promises of heaven are used only rarely, if ever, in the Bible as the basis for urging faithfulness to God, however. Far more prevalent are attempts to speak of the end as a way of presenting "how things ought to be" and "how things will be." That is, end-time images are designed as an antidote to the myopia that threatens us, those of us whose horizons of meaning are determined by a fallen world.

---

[8]E.g., Rev. 1:4; 2:13; 3:21; 4—5; 6:16; 7:9; et al.

Let us return to the book of Revelation. In chapters 4 and 5, John the Seer is led into the throne room of God in order to acquire a fresh, heavenly perspective from which to understand reality. There, he is ushered into the backstage of history, so to speak, behind the curtains, so as to see what is really going on in his world, and in the world of his audience. In time, he will also be given a vision of the end, so that he can see the present from the perspective of God's ultimate purpose for the cosmos. In this way, his worldview is exploded, and the vision he records in his Revelation is nothing less than an assault on his readers' everyday categories of meaning. Their sights are opened to the world beyond the world—that is, to the transcendent, the unseen work of God. They are exposed to an alternative portrait of their world, and the effect is two competing visions: reality from God's perspective, and the view of the world propagated by imperial Rome. Suddenly, the almighty power of Rome is unmasked as deceitful and anemic, capable of being resisted.

> In heaven and from the perspective of heaven John sees what is ultimately the truth of reality: who God really is, what God's purpose for his whole creation is, and how God is accomplishing that purpose through Jesus, the Spirit, and the church. From a merely earthly perspective, the military and political might of imperial Rome (the beast) and the economic dominance of the city of Rome (Babylon) seem irresistible, even divine. But from the perspective of heaven the ultimacy Roman propaganda claimed for Rome is seen to be illusory. The reign of the evil powers who appear to contest God's sovereignty on earth so successfully is neither ultimate (in heaven God reigns over all) nor eternal (God's rule must come on earth as it already is in heaven).[9]

In short, Revelation is concerned with a conversion of the imagination.

End-time thinking more generally in scripture has this primary focus, to push the boundaries of what is real and what is possible. As Paul Ricoeur has described it, imagination has to do with what we allow to count as real, so that to transform the imagination is to transform human existence. Thus, "if you want to change a people's

---

[9]Richard Bauckham, "The Relevance of Revelation," *Catalyst* 24 (4, 1996): 1–3 (1).

obedience, you must change their imagination."[10] Expanded horizons have as their corollary fresh allegiances and practices in the world. Those who adopt Revelation's perspective on the cosmos will be transformed in their dispositions, and will behave in ways appropriate to the world as God has thus revealed it to be. In the case of Revelation, this means that evil is neither to be feared nor served, but resisted and destroyed. The kingdom of God will be actualized through the victory of the Lion-Lamb (Rev. 5), whose faithful witness to the point of sacrificial death stands as the measure of the faithfulness of those who would serve the in-breaking dominion of God. In this way, end-time thinking serves as a call to march according to the drumbeat of a distant, future drummer. It is to begin the performance of a script that is clear in its basic parts but still in the process of being written, and which actually belongs to a future time and place. It is to live "as if" God's rule were fully present, and so to see with the eyes of faith those things not otherwise seen. (Compare Heb. 11:1.)

End-time talk serves also to remind God's people that the church is a work in progress, and that salvation itself is a process. For this reason, Paul can refer to Christians as those "who are being saved" (1 Cor. 1:18; 2 Cor. 2:15). In a passage remarkable for its profundity and brevity, Peter can characterize salvation in three tenses—past, present, and future: "By his great mercy he has given us a new birth into a living hope through the resurrection of Jesus Christ from the dead, and into an inheritance that is imperishable, undefiled, and unfading, kept in heaven for you, who are being protected by the power of God through faith for a salvation ready to be revealed in the last time" (1 Pet. 1:3–5). That is, the gift of the new birth rests in Christ's resurrection (past); the work of salvation is ongoing as believers are "protected by the power of God" (present); and God's work of salvation will be consummated ("revealed in the last time," future). Other New Testament texts illustrate how widespread is this way of thinking about salvation in its past, present, and future tenses: "Therefore, since we are justified by faith, we have peace with God through our Lord Jesus Christ, through whom we have obtained access to this grace in which we stand; and we boast in our hope of sharing

---

[10]Paul Ricoeur, cited in "Reflections," *Christianity Today* (7 February 2000): 84. See the helpful summary in Kevin J. Vanhoozer, *Biblical Narrative in the Philosophy of Paul Ricoeur: A Study in Hermeneutics and Theology* (Cambridge: Cambridge Univ. Press, 1990), esp. 23–25.

the glory of God" (Rom. 5:1–2). "So if you have been raised with Christ, seek the things that are above, where Christ is, seated at the right hand of God. Set your minds on things that are above, not on things that are on earth, for you have died, and your life is hidden with Christ in God. When Christ who is your life is revealed, then you also will be revealed with him in glory" (Col. 3:1–4). Salvation is a reality accomplished in the past, an ongoing, present experience, and an achievement still anticipated.

These ruminations invite further clarity on two points: the currency of salvation and the nature of future salvation.

The Currency of Salvation

In the last chapter, we noted that the grace of God invites on the part of humans a response of conversion—that is, a realignment of one's deepest commitments and dispositions toward the purpose of God. This involves repentance and belief, but these mark only the onset of the journey. Simon Peter, James, and John may recognize their sinfulness, they may receive Jesus' call to join him in "catching people," and they may leave everything to follow him (Lk. 5:1–11), for example, but in an important sense this "conversion" is only the beginning. Jesus goes on to instruct these and other disciples in the dispositions and practices appropriate to the converted life (especially Lk. 6:12–49). Yet they show little understanding of the character of his mission (for example, Lk. 9) and seem very little to share in his grasp of God's purpose and work; have they genuinely been converted? In fact, just before the beginning of the lengthy journey to Jerusalem (Lk. 9:51—19:48), Luke says of the disciples, "They did not understand what Jesus was saying; its meaning was concealed from them, so that they could not perceive it" (Lk. 9:45, author's translation). This is not because God concealed from them Jesus' significance; after all, the disciples are those to whom the secrets of the kingdom have been revealed (Lk. 8:10), and Jesus assumes that they should be able to understand his words (Lk. 9:44a). Rather, in spite of their conversion and experience thus far with Jesus, they remain too much in the clutches of old ways of reckoning God's ways, old allegiances, and old values. They cannot grasp Jesus' words because they lack the necessary categories of thought. The horizons of what they regard as possible, even for God, are still too limiting. What is more, even at the close of the lengthy period of instruction narrated

in the central, journey section of Luke's gospel (9:51—19:48), in which
the formation of the disciples is a paramount concern, Luke records
again that "they understood nothing about all these things..., and
they did not grasp what was said" (Lk. 18:34). Apparently, salvation
is an ongoing process of illumination, forming, cleansing. Indeed,
discipleship as Luke develops it entails a reconstruction of one's self
within a new web of relationships, a transfer of allegiances, and the
embodiment of transformed dispositions and attitudes. Such a
conversion requires re-socialization within the community being
formed around Jesus, and this is a process that continues for these
disciples even beyond the gospel narrative itself.

This is not a perspective unique to Luke, of course.[11] Paul's
recognition that the Thessalonian Christians had turned from idols
to serve the living and true God (1 Thess. 1:9–10) is written in
deceptively simple terms. In reality, Paul thus speaks *at least* of a transfer
of allegiances, a relocation of social relations, a reformation of
theological categories, fresh habits and behaviors, and a recalculation
of one's place in the socio-political world of Thessalonika. Now they
inhabit a new social space, living "between the times"; having converted
to the living God, anticipating the coming of Jesus, they now make
their lives in a period of active waiting. In the interim, God's word is
"at work" in these believers, just as Paul calls upon them "to lead a life
worthy of God" (1 Thess. 2:11–13). Growing in grace through the
Holy Spirit that dwells in them, they are "more and more" to comport
themselves in the world in ways consistent with their having been set
apart for service to God (1 Thess. 4:1–17). Indeed, Paul's prayer is
that "the God of peace himself sanctify you entirely" so that they
might "be kept sound and blameless at the coming of our Lord Jesus
Christ" (1 Thess. 5:23).

For Paul, the present bestowal of the Spirit on believers is a sign
of the coming of the end and the means by which believers are being
conformed to the life of salvation. In Romans 8:23, he refers to the
Spirit as "first fruits," an agricultural image found in the Old
Testament: the first of the harvest, with more certainly to come. The
Spirit is also for Paul the guarantee, a kind of down payment providing

---

[11]See the helpful discussion in Wayne A. Meeks, *The Origins of Christian Morality: The First Two Centuries* (New Haven, Conn.: Yale Univ. Press, 1993), 18–36.

assurance of the consummation of God's redemptive work (2 Cor. 1:22; 5:5; compare Eph. 1:14). The Christian life as a whole is described as walking "in" or "according to" the Spirit (Rom. 8:4, 9), and it is the indwelling Spirit who produces in the lives of believers the characteristic dispositions and behaviors of Christians: love, joy, peace, patience, and the rest (Gal. 5:22–23).

The motif of progress in salvation can be traced endlessly in scripture. Paul's confidence among the Philippians is "that the one who began a good work among you will bring it to completion by the day of Jesus Christ" (Phil. 1:6). Metaphors drawn from the building trade, athletic competition, journeying, human development, and agriculture are all put into play in the service of encouraging Christian growth. "Like newborn infants, long for the pure, spiritual milk, so that by it you may grow into salvation" (1 Pet. 2:2). "So let us not grow weary in doing what is right, for we will reap at harvest time, if we do not give up" (Gal. 6:9). "Now if anyone builds on the foundation with gold, silver, precious stones, wood, hay, straw—the work of each builder will become visible, for the Day will disclose it, because it will be revealed with fire, and the fire will test what sort of work each has done" (1 Cor. 3:12–13). For Luke, the community of Jesus' followers are known as "the Way" (Acts 9:2; 19:23; 22:4), a metaphor drawn from the new exodus imagery of Isaiah—"Prepare the way of the Lord!" (Isa. 40:3; Lk. 3:4)—signifying their commitment to the way of salvation. Paul marks the Christian life as one of progress in his favorite expression for this life, the "walk" (for example, Rom. 6:4; 8:4; 2 Cor. 5:7).

Because it holds together the whole history of God's purpose in creation, Colossians 3:9–11 is of special interest: "You have stripped off the old self with its practices and have clothed yourselves with the new self, which is being renewed in knowledge according to the image of its creator. In that renewal there is no longer Greek and Jew, circumcised and uncircumcised, barbarian, Scythian, slave and free; but Christ is all and in all!" The new humanity ushered in with the advent of Christ is one that eschews those distinctions that would have splintered Roman society. This vision has its foundation in creation, in God's act to make humanity, male and female, in God's own image. Here, however, Paul takes the added step of noting that *the creation of humanity in God's image is an ongoing process.* This "image," in order to remain ever new, must have continuous contact with the one whose image it is, the Creator, who, in the christology of Colossians, is none other than Christ (Col. 1:15).[12] This "image" entails an obviously corporate dimension, with immediate implications for how those who follow Christ engage in relations with other persons, and especially for how they breach those socio-religious, cultural, and national barriers that segregate people. Those who are saved engage in an ongoing process whereby they frame their social relations and behavior in ways that nurture day-to-day renewal in their insight into, and reflection of, the character and purpose of God.

Just as the story of the Bible has a beginning, middle, and end, so has the story of personal salvation. From the beginning of the conversion, the end is in view, to which the letter of Ephesians refers as "the unity of the faith and of the knowledge of the Son of God"— that is, "maturity," "the measure of the full stature of Christ" (Eph. 4:13). Between these two points, beginning and end, is the process of growth, walking "in newness of life" (Rom. 6:4), the ongoing present-ness of salvation.

The Nature of Future Salvation

The consummation of salvation lies in the future. Scripture provides tantalizing glimpses of its character, and is adamant both that it is in that future that our hope lies and that our present should be worked out in relation to that future. The witness of the biblical materials on this point is multifaceted and any attempt to summarize will be unavoidably selective and incomplete. The list of pertinent issues would include the following:[13]

(1) It is an embodied life. According to the famous Roman orator Cicero (106–43 B.C.E.), the two primary answers to the question: "What happens when we die?" were these: either the body and soul are annihilated at death or the soul separates from the body.[14] Other views are known in the Roman world, and, in ancient Corinth, these differences help to explain disunity among the Christian believers. In Paul's talk of "the waking of the dead," some would have heard echoes of fables about the resuscitation of corpses, the stuff of popular myths.

---

[12]Cf. James D.G. Dunn, *The Epistles to the Colossians and to Philemon*, New International Greek Testament Commentary (Grand Rapids, Mich.: Wm. B. Eerdmans, 1996), 222.

[13]Cf. Murray J. Harris, "Salvation," in *New Dictionary of Biblical Theology*, ed. T. Desmond Alexander and Brian S. Rosner (Downers Grove, Ill.: InterVarsity, 2000), 762–67 (766).

[14]Cicero *Tusculan Disputations* 1.11.23–24.

This would have included those who possessed the wherewithal to entertain traveling philosophers, who would have had some awareness of the philosophical categories current in the Empire. Taught generally to degrade the body, they would have found Paul's teaching about the resurrection incomprehensible, even ridiculous. Others, who would not have had access to the influence of itinerant philosophers, would have had closer contact with superstitions and popular myths, including those relating the resuscitation of corpses and the endowment of those corpses with immortality. Since Paul's primary objective in 1 Corinthians is to restore unity (1 Cor. 1:10), his particular challenge in 1 Corinthians 15 is to represent the resurrection belief of early Christianity with enough sophistication to communicate effectively with all sides.

Paul defends belief in the future resurrection by (1) appealing to what had already become Christian tradition (1 Cor. 15:1–11), (2) observing that a denial of the future resurrection was tantamount to denying the resurrection of Christ, and moving on to an affirmation of Christ's resurrection as "first fruits" of the future resurrection (1 Cor. 15:12–34), and (3) sketching how one might plausibly conceive of the resurrection of the dead (1 Cor. 15:35–58). Crucial for our purposes in this chapter is Paul's central affirmation of the import of the body to human existence and identity, and, then, of God's provision of a body well-suited to the form of existence envisioned.

How can Paul speak of eternal, *embodied* existence, when it is self-evident that our bodies are fragile and susceptible to disease and death? By way of reply, Paul introduces a distinction between two sorts of body—one oriented toward life in this world (*sōma psychikon*), the other oriented toward life in the world to come (*sōma pneumatikon*). The first is drawn from Genesis 2:7, which has it that Adam was created a living being (*psychē*); hence, the first Adam had a body fit for life in this world. However, this body is ill-suited to eternal life with God, subject as it is to death and decay on account of sin. What is needed, then, is a different form of existence, which is given us by the last Adam, Christ, who does not simply receive life (as in the first Adam), but actually gives it. As a consequence, this second body is one fit for the age to come.

Thus, in 1 Corinthians 15:38–58 Paul affirms the following about resurrection life. (1) There is a nonnegotiable continuity between present life in this world and life everlasting with God. For human beings, this continuity has to do with bodily existence. Paul cannot think in terms of a free-floating soul separate from a body. (2) Present human existence is marked by frailty, deterioration, weakness, and is therefore unsuited for eternal life. Therefore, in order for Christian believers to share in eternal life, their bodies must be transformed. Paul does not here think of "immortality of the soul," nor does he proclaim a resuscitation of dead bodies that might serve as receptacles for souls that had escaped the body in death. Instead, he sets before his audience the promise of the transformation of their bodies. (Compare Phil. 3:21.) (3) For Paul, this is consequential for the nature of Christian life in the present. For example, this message underscores the significance of life in this world—a fact that many Christians at Corinth had not taken seriously. We should not imagine that our bodies are unimportant, then, or that what we do to our bodies or with our bodies is somehow unrelated to eternal life. (Compare Col. 1:24.) The idea of eternal life is not "escapism." Rather, it provides the Christian both with hope as well as with a vision of what is important to God.

(2) *It is a personal, social life that embraces human diversity.* Unlike the perspective of some religions, including the gnostic teachings that would attract some Christians in the centuries immediately after the era of the New Testament, for biblical faith the life of the coming age is not one in which persons are absorbed into God's being, or into some sort of primordial spirit. Nor is this future life one that obliterates human distinctiveness in favor of sameness. True, the distinction between Jew and Gentile has been overcome, so that God's people, Jew and Gentile, are united in peace (Eph. 2:11–22; Gal. 6:15–16). But John's vision of the heavenly chorus has it that "there was a great multitude that no one could count, from every nation, from all tribes and peoples and languages, standing before the throne and before the Lamb, robed in white, with palm branches in their hands. They cried out in a loud voice, saying, 'Salvation belongs to our God who is seated on the throne, and to the Lamb!'" (Rev. 7:9–10). So, while the divide between Jew and Gentile has become obsolete "in Christ," and while individual rivalry has no place in the world to come, the new humanity should not be thought of as a heavenly melting pot. John's vision points to the fulfillment of God's promise to Abraham, that he would have innumerable descendants—"like the dust of the earth" (Gen. 13:16), as many as the stars in the sky (Gen. 15:5), too many

to count (Gen. 16:10), "as the sand that is on the seashore" (Gen. 22:17)—a father of *many nations* and not of a single people (Gen. 17:4–6).

(3) It is eternal life. It follows that the transitory character of present life contrasts sharply with the nature of the life to come. John speaks of the blessings of salvation as eternal life, which for him begins with faith in Christ and continues beyond death into the eschaton (for example, Jn. 3:15–16, 36; 5:24). The seer speaks of the heavenly reign of God's people "forever and ever" (Rev. 22:5). For Paul, this is not because anything about the human person is immortal. In 1 Corinthians 15 and in 2 Corinthians 5:1–10, he affirms that transformation and immortality are the consequence of (and not preparation for) resurrection.[15]

(4) It is life in a restored cosmos. Paul actually employs the phrase "new creation" in 2 Corinthians 5:17 and Galatians 6:15, and uses a related expression, "new humanity," in Ephesians 2:15; 4:23–24; and Colossians 3:9–10 (last two, author's translation). These terms have roots in Second Temple Judaism, where they speak to the expectation of the restoration of the entire creation, which now exists in a state of futility on account of human sin. The fertile ground for these ideas can be found in Isaiah 56—66, with its promise of a new heaven and new earth. The end would embrace the original goodness of God's creation, but also extend beyond the original to a cosmos that would continue into eternity in its restored state. New life includes all things. (See Rom. 8:18–25; 1 Cor. 15:24–28; 2 Cor. 5:16–18; Phil. 3:21; Col. 1:15–20; Eph. 1:10.)

(5) It is life ushered in by the coming of Christ. It is clear that, as a whole, the New Testament writers anticipated a decisive act of God to bring the purpose of history to its close, and that this end would be ushered in by the coming of Jesus Christ. Hebrews actually uses the language of a "second" coming: "Christ, having been offered once to bear the sins of many, will appear a second time, not to deal with sin, but to save those who are eagerly waiting for him" (9:28), whereas other witnesses speak of the "the revealing" of Christ (for example, 1 Cor. 1:7) or even long prayerfully for his coming: "Our Lord, come!" (1 Cor. 16:22), "Come, Lord Jesus!" (Rev. 22:20). "Strengthen your

---

[15]Cf. Richard N. Longenecker, "Is There Development in Paul's Resurrection Thought?" in *Life in the Face of Death: The Resurrection Message of the New Testament*, McMaster New Testament Series (Grand Rapids, Mich.: Wm. B. Eerdmans, 1998), 171–202.

hearts, for the coming of the Lord is near" (Jas. 5:8). "The Lord is near" (Phil. 4:5).

Such language can be used as motivation for ethical excellence, of course. More often than not, however, these statements of hope and anticipation are more pointedly focused on putting current life in perspective and on reminding God's people that their beginning and end is in the peaceful joy of God's righteous presence. The final vision of Revelation 21—22 has God no longer occupying a heavenly throne, but actually making a home on earth, with humanity. The terms John uses to describe this apparent innovation actually speak to ancient realities. God "will dwell with them," the NRSV translates, but we might more literally say that God "will make a tent with them," just as God's presence was with Israel in the tabernacle of the exodus journey and in the temple. God present with people in holiness and glory—in the end, this is what makes the "new heaven" and the "new earth" authentically "new," for it is God's presence that generates and nurtures new creation. As God is the Alpha and the Omega, the One "who lives forever and ever" (Rev. 4:9, 10; 10:6; 15:7), so the new life God gives is life in its most full sense: life in and beyond the hazards and forces that mar present existence, life in the embrace of the unmediated loving care of God, forever.

The Community of Salvation in Acts

What is the role of the community of God's people in work of salvation? Simply put, the church, which owes its very existence and purpose to the coming of salvation, is that people who, together, embody, nurture, and propagate this salvation. Just as Israel has its origins as a holy nation in the gracious election and powerful intervention of God in the exodus, so the church traces its beginnings to the restoration of Israel in the gracious intervention of God in the birth, life, ministry, death, and resurrection of Jesus. Among the New Testament writings, the book of Acts, itself a narrative of salvation, is most oriented toward helping us gain our bearings in this regard.

In the gospel of Luke and the Acts of the Apostles, the language of salvation is especially significant and, in narrative terms, it is easy to see that salvation is that theme around which all other ele-ments of Luke's work are oriented.[16] In the context of Acts, above all else,

[16]In Acts, see 2:21, 40, 47; 3:16; 4:9, 12, 14; 5:16, 31; 7:10, 25, 34; 8:7; 9:34; 10:38; 11:14; 12:11; 13:23, 26, 47; 14:9; 15:1, 11; 16:30, 31; 17:25; 23:24, 27; 26:17; 27:20, 31, 34, 43, 44; 28:1, 4, 8, 9, 27, 28.

salvation signifies incorporation into and participation in the Christ-centered community of God's people. In this case, the term "community" must be taken in its most radical sense, as Luke repeatedly underscores the prayerful unity and concord of these persons, with their oneness embodied in a vivid way through their economic sharing (for example, 1:14; 2:1, 44–45; 4:31—5:11). Their oneness is focused on their common relation to Christ, in whose name they heal (3:6, 16; 4:10, 30; 19:13), preach (4:12; 5:28, 40), and are baptized (2:38; 4:10, 30; 8:16; 19:13); they suffer for his name (5:41; 9:16; 21:13), and are those who call upon the name of the Lord Jesus (2:21, 36; 9:14, 21; 22:16).

In Luke's narrative, baptism is both response and gift. That is, offering oneself to baptism is one of the prescribed ways of responding to the message of salvation, a public "turning" to God as God is revealed in the coming of Christ. But baptism is also one of the blessings of salvation. As the community of God's people discerns God's acceptance of persons, they are incorporated into the community through the rite of baptism, signifying forgiveness and acceptance. Water-baptism and Spirit-baptism are correlated in Acts, though not in terms of simple priority of order, as though one must occur before the other. Instead, they are viewed as interrelated community and divine responses to human repentance. It is through the gift of the Spirit that God proves in Acts to be the savior of Jew and Gentile alike. By pouring upon the Gentiles the blessing of forgiveness and the gift of the Spirit, God testifies to the authenticity of their membership in the community of God's people and, "in cleansing their hearts by faith," God confirms that "he has made no distinction between them and us" (15:7–9; compare 11:15–18). In baptism, then, the community of God's people recognizes and affirms the gracious work of God, even among those regarded by many as beyond the reach of God's grace.

Before getting further ahead of ourselves, we should also observe that Luke sketches the content of salvation in two other ways: as forgiveness of sins and as the reception of the Holy Spirit. Indeed, Peter promises that the effect of undergoing a repentance-baptism is that "your sins may be forgiven; and you will receive the gift of the Holy Spirit" (Acts 2:38). Elsewhere in Acts, "forgiveness" can function as a virtual stand-in for the whole of salvation's blessings. (See 5:31; 13:26, 28; 4:10–12; 10:43; 11:14.) Forgiveness marks a new/renewed relationship with God, of course, but also with God's people, and points to God's gathering the restored people of God. The same could be said of the gift of the Spirit, since the outpouring of the Spirit was promised by Joel (2:28–32) as the centerpiece of the end-time restoration of Israel from exile. That the gift of the Spirit helps to define salvation in Acts is self-evident in the narrative of Pentecost in Acts 2, but this emphasis comes to the surface again and again in the ensuing narrative (for example, 9:17; 10:43–44; 11:15–17; 15:8). Quite apart from any self-understanding or strategic thinking on the part of the community, the Spirit is poured out on those who respond to the good news, signifying both the restoration of Israel and, more to the present point, that these persons have been embraced as God's restored people.

Christology and Preaching

For Luke, these emphases are tied together with christology and with the proclamation of those first Christians. Central to both was news of Jesus' resurrection. For example, in the first public address recounted in Acts, Peter affirms Jesus' status as Lord and Christ with reference to his resurrection. Of course, from this perspective Jesus *becomes* nothing at the resurrection that he was not already; at his birth the angels declare that he is Savior, Messiah, and Lord (Lk. 2:11). During his ministry, however, the exalted status of Jesus signified by these titles was not understood even by his followers. Moreover, it was rejected by the Jerusalem elite who were instrumental in bringing about what must have been regarded as decisive proof against Jesus' exalted status—namely, his execution on a Roman cross. Jesus' resurrection thus serves to validate the status Jesus possessed already, but which was in doubt on account of his maltreatment in Jerusalem. In Peter's Pentecost sermon, the proof of Jesus' resurrection comes in three parts: (1) David the prophet anticipated Jesus' resurrection and enthronement as Messiah (Acts 2:25–31); (2) Peter and the other apostles are themselves witnesses of Jesus' resurrection (Acts 2:32); and (3) the phenomena associated with the outpouring of the Spirit ("what you yourselves see and hear," author's translation) are the consequence of Jesus' exaltation and reception of the promise of the Spirit (Acts 2:33). The christology of Peter's sermon is marked by God's irrefutable vindication of Jesus' identity, even to the point that Jesus is now regarded as coregent with God in the gracious provision of the blessings of salvation.

Shortly thereafter, Peter and John are brought up on charges for this very message—that is, for "proclaiming that in Jesus there is the resurrection of the dead" (Acts 4:2). Note that their message was not simply that Jesus had been raised, but rather that in Jesus there is resurrection. This presses the question, what is "resurrection"?

The idea of resurrection from the dead does not pervade the Old Testament, but appears in the latter years of Israel's faith, with hints of resurrection faith appearing in only a handful of prophetic texts. For example, in Hosea 6:1–3 we read of the prospect of the revival of God's people:

"Come, let us return to the LORD;
for it is he who has torn, and he will heal us;
    he has struck down, and he will bind us up.
After two days he will revive us;
    on the third day he will raise us up,
    that we may live before him.
Let us know, let us press on to know the LORD;
    his appearing is as sure as the dawn;
he will come to us like the showers,
    like the spring rains that water the earth."

This prophecy attracted the attention of the church fathers, who read in it a prophecy of Jesus' resurrection on the third day, and early Jewish interpretation found here a reference to the end-time resurrection of Israel. In its own eighth-century B.C.E. context, however, this "raising up" is more likely to refer metaphorically to the restoration of the nation. Ezekiel 37:1–14, with its dramatic image of the valley of dry bones brought to life, also provides a vision of Israel's restoration. This did not keep later Jewish interpretation from finding there a graphic depiction of the resurrection, however. Note especially verses 12–13: "I am going to bring you up from your graves." In both of these texts, we find the interweaving of the promise of Israel's restoration with the re-creative work of the Lord.

Many scholars find a more direct reference to resurrection in Isaiah 26:19:

Your dead shall live, their corpses shall rise.
    O dwellers in the dust, awake and sing for joy!
For your dew is a radiant dew,
    and the earth will give birth to those long dead.

Like the vision in Ezekiel 37, Isaiah's words appear in a context that proposes Israel's restoration and, indeed, exaltation among the nations. With regard to the meaning of this text in particular, the debate centers on whether a literal raising up of dead corpses is envisioned. At the very least, however, we have here in Isaiah a further text that relates the notion of resurrection to the activity by which God restores and exalts the people, and pours upon them the totality of covenant blessings.

The first unambiguous reference to the physical resurrection of the dead appears in Daniel 12:1–3:

> At that time Michael, the great prince, the protector of your people, shall arise. There shall be a time of anguish, such as has never occurred since nations first came into existence. But at that time your people shall be delivered, everyone who is found written in the book. Many of those who sleep in the dust of the earth shall awake, some to everlasting life, and some to shame and everlasting contempt. Those who are wise shall shine like the brightness of the sky, and those who lead many to righteousness, like the stars forever and ever.

This passage forms the climax of the revelation that began in Daniel 11:2, and marks the decisive triumph of God's people over the enemies of Israel. At last, Israel will experience salvation in its fullest sense. Not all will experience this deliverance, however, but only those found in "the book" (that is, the book of life—compare Isa. 4:3; Mal. 3:16–18). Others will experience the resurrection as judgment. It is in this way that Daniel's concern with the vindication of God's righteous servants comes into clearest focus.

When we take these texts into account, together with additional Jewish material written in the era of the Second Temple, several motifs begin to surface, and these help us to know what categories of interpretation might have been available to those who first heard of Jesus' resurrection: (1) Resurrection signals the restoration of Israel. (2) Resurrection signals Israel's triumph over its enemies. (3) Resurrection marks God's vindication of the righteous who have suffered unjustly. Having been condemned and made to suffer by a human court, the righteous will in the resurrection be vindicated in the divine court. (4) Resurrection marks the decisive establishment of divine justice, where rewards and punishments are meted out in relation to the character of one's life before death. Injustice and wickedness will not have the final word, but in the resurrection will be decisively repudiated.

To return to the indictment brought against the apostles in Acts 4, then, their proclamation of "resurrection" was tantamount to their announcement of the restoration of Israel under God's rule. And for the Jewish elite, who drew their authority and stature from the status quo under Roman rule, this could hardly have been "good news."

Against this backdrop, the book of Acts proclaims salvation as the end-time restoration of Israel, intimately correlating the resurrection and exaltation of Jesus with Jesus' role in the outpouring of the Spirit. What are the effects of this message for the life of the church? For the narrative of Acts, these would include:

- The Holy Spirit creates and forms the community of God's people, so that the characteristic behaviors of Jesus' followers, as sketched in Acts 2:42–47 (for example, prayer, worship, economic sharing, common meals) must be regarded as the work of the Spirit within God's people;[17]
- The community created by the Spirit is none other than the people of Abraham, Isaac, and Jacob (for example, 3:13; 7:8, 32), signifying in a crucial sense that God's purpose is one and, therefore, God's people, across time and space, is one. Israel's story is the church's story and, then, their story is our story, just as their God is our God;
- The Holy Spirit empowers and directs this community for mission, moving the people of God beyond long-established and taken-for-granted religio-ethnic barriers to "the ends of the earth" (1:8; compare, for example, chapters 8, 16; 10:1— 11:18), so that the contours of the mission itself comprise a profound statement about the social ramifications of the message of salvation;
- The mission of the church serves to propagate the message that God's redemptive purpose is being actualized in the world. Evangelism, then, is the announcement in word and deed: The times have changed! These are the days of "resurrection"! And this changing of the aeons calls for a radical reordering of life (for example, 3:12–26; 17:30–31);

---

[17]Cf. Matthias Wenk, *Community-forming Power: The Socio-Ethical Role of the Spirit in Luke-Acts,* Journal of Pentecostal Theology Supplement Series 19 (Sheffield: Sheffield Academic Press, 2000).

- The message of resurrection is explicitly realized in the life of God's people in their extending hospitality, their economic sharing, and otherwise their ensuring that "there was not a needy person among them" (4:32–35). In this and other ways, the community of God's people embodies the reign of God and cares for as well as socializes its members with respect to the ongoing experience and hope of salvation;
- The content of preaching serves the purpose of preaching— namely, to assault the imaginations of people, to press the boundaries of what people will allow as possible, in order to grasp in fresh ways the character of God's work in the world. The story of God's history with Israel must be told and retold (for example, Acts 7; 13:16–41), but only as interpreted correctly, in continuity with the exaltation of Jesus by God and, thus, in relation to the actualization of God's purpose in Christ and through the church, then and now; and
- The common life of the church, its determination in the face of persecution, and the direction of the mission are set within the arena of worship (2:42–47; 4:24–30; 10:9, 33; 11:18; 13:2). The centrality of worship can scarcely be overstated, given that it is precisely in relation to the worship of God that the community opens itself to a vision of reality that counters the dominant ideology of their daily experience otherwise. Worship in this case is not other-worldly in the sense of withdrawal from the world, but an acknowledgment of the God of Israel, the living God, whose purpose and work in the world set the agenda for those who would serve, and not hinder, God. In worship, God's people refresh their grasp on how things ought to be, focus on God's perspective and saving project, and align themselves with God's aims.

In these and other ways, the community of God's people is the community of salvation.

Had we stepped outside of the Acts of the Apostles for this overview, we would have found similar materials, sometimes with different emphases. For example, a closer examination of Paul would have brought to our attention the importance of the Last Supper in the definition of the church; God's people, if they take seriously the selfless, sacrificial act of Christ on the cross, will embody servanthood and sacrifice in their common life "until he comes" (1 Cor. 11:17–34).

Another example: The hymnody of the book of Revelation would have underscored for us even more the importance of worship in the projection and maintenance of a full-orbed vision of God's work, over against that perspective on reality inspired and broadcast by the beast, in the service of the dragon. Worship, in this instance, would have served even more as an act of rehearsal in anticipation of things to come, and as an act of proclamation of the world's goal and future.[18] But, already, we have identified important landmarks for the journey of the community of salvation.

Epilogue

The character of the message of salvation and its contemporary embodiment are inescapably determined by the end. This, at least, is the witness of scripture, however unpalatable it may seem to those more accustomed to living for today, and however distasteful it might be to those of us who have grown weary of end-time sensationalism. The message of salvation runs like a thread through the whole of scripture, from Genesis to Revelation, and participates integrally in how we understand the beginning, middle, and end of the biblical story. As with narratives more generally, so this one goes unfulfilled, it fails its purpose, if it is reduced to one aspect of its plot or another. The end shapes the beginning and middle. Perhaps even more so, this narrative fails its purpose if we find ourselves willing "to figure it out" apart from personal engagement and consequences. This narrative, above all narratives, invites active participation. "Come," it beckons, as it seeks a people to dwell in its story, to have their lives determined decisively by it.

What are the consequences of an engaged reading of this scripture, and of our "being read" by it? In this chapter, we have highlighted several effects. First, and perhaps most profoundly, this is not all there is. Our experience of life in the world is a chapter, for us a very important one, but it is not the whole book. For some, this will come as a word of comfort and delight. This is because it urges us to place sometimes horrific images of suffering and tragedy within the larger mural of a God who can turn mourning into dancing (Ps. 30:11), who wipes away the tears (Rev. 21:4). For others, this will come as a

---

[18]Justo L. González, *For the Healing of the Nations: The Book of Revelation in an Age of Cultural Conflict* (Maryknoll, N.Y.: Orbis, 1999), 107–12.

stunning surprise and warning, a resounding charge against the pretensions of human efforts. If consciously placed within the grand sweep of history in God's care, much of what concerns us now would pale in significance.

Second, the end casts its shadow backward on present existence, giving us perspective on what will be and, thus, what ought to be. On the one hand, this means that visions of the end serve to expand the horizons of what we allow and take to be true and important. Immersing ourselves in these biblical materials, and immersing ourselves in worship shaped by this end-time perspective, in turn shapes us, transforming our life-worlds and, thus, our allegiances and practices. On the other hand, then, when the end back-shadows its interests into our worlds, it does so in order to generate a crisis in our lives, calling for response. Things are not the way they are supposed to be. We serve the present age by serving the consummation of all things, by getting in sync with God's project and practices in bringing creation to its real purpose. In this way, as the community of God's people, we come to embody God's salvation, as well as take on the role of agents of salvation. (See 2 Cor. 5:18–20.)

Third, we come face to face with the reality that we who comprise the community of the saved are "in process." Our past is firmly enmeshed in the redemptive acts of God, in exodus and in Christ. Our future is secured in God's sovereign purpose, guaranteed by the empowering presence of the Holy Spirit. Our present is part of God's work, too. The metaphors abound: growing up in Christ, clothing ourselves in Christ, producing the Spirit's fruit, and more. These signify the imperative of pressing onward, toward Christlikeness, in the awareness that it is Christ who demonstrates for us what it means to reflect in our lives the very image of God. For this we were made, and are now being remade. Like Paul, we have not yet attained the intimacy with Christ Jesus and the transformation into Christlikeness for which Christ has made us his own. But we press on toward this goal, which is ours in Christ (Phil. 3:10–14).

SCRIPTURE INDEX

GENESIS

1	9–10, 19–21
1—2	15, 18
1:2	83
1:6–9	83
1:22	18
1:26	18
1:26–27	40
1:26–28	15
1:27	18–20
1:28	18, 28
1:30	18, 22
1:31	10, 15
2:4–9	15–16
2:7	22, 134
2:8–9	23–24
2:9	25
2:15–25	15–16
2:17	26
2:18	18
2:19–20	25
3	20, 23–29, 53
3:1	25
3:1–9	24
3:1–15	81
3:3	27
3:5	25
3:6	25, 26
3:7	25
4:1–16	28
4:17–24	28
5:1–3	20
5:28–29	28
6:1—9:18	28
8:1–3	83
9:5–6	20
9:7	28
9:17–27	28
11	28
11:6–9	28

12:2	67
12:7	67
13:14–17	67
13:16	135
15:5	67, 135
15:13–14	66
15:18	67
16:10	136
17:4–5	74
17:4–6	136
18:18	67
22:17	136
37—50	67
38:1–26	57
49:25	18
50:17	55
50:20	67

EXODUS

1:1–9	67
1:10–11	67
1:22	67
2:23	67
3:1—4:17	96
3:8	68–69
3:14	66, 82–83
3:17	69
4:12	96
4:23	68
6:6	68–69, 111
6:7	67
7:3	47
7:16	68
8:1	68
8:19	84
9:1	68
9:13	68
10:3	68
10:17	55
10:26	68

13:3	68
13:15	69
13:21	96
14:12	68
14:19	96
14:24	82, 96
14:30	5, 68
15	74
15:1	68
15:1–13	69–70
15:3	74
15:10	81
15:13	69
15:18	70
15:21	45
15:25	45
15:26	44–45
16:13	111
18:4	18
19:1–6	77
19:5–6	91
19:6	59
19:9	96
19:16	96
20:2	66
24:8	100
25—31	96
25:22	96
29—30	96
29:10	100
29:15	100
29:19–20	100
29:46	66
32:9	94
33:3	94
33:9	96
34:6	82
40:34	96

LEVITICUS

1—7	98
3:2	100

3:8	100
3:13	100
4:1—6:7	98
6:24—7:10	98
11:45	58, 66
13—14	42–43, 109
14:14	100
16	98
16:22	98–99
19	58–59
19:18	87
19:22	99
19:36	66
22:33	66
25:38	66
26:13	66

NUMBERS

2	65
14:40	28
15:41	66
21	110
21:7	28
23:22	66
24:8	66

DEUTERONOMY

1:30	66
4:34	47
5:6	66
6:5	22
6:13	76
6:16	76
7:8	77
7:19	47
8:3	76
8:14	66
9:26	77
10:12	68
10:16	94
13:5	66
18:15–18	75
23:14	96
25:5–10	57
26:5–9	70
26:5–10	67

26:8	47
28	43
29:3	47
32:5	94
32:36–39	46
32:39	46
34:11	47

JOSHUA

3—4	73
5:13–15	64
7:20	28
9	64

JUDGES

6:24	58
7:2	65
10:10	28
10:15	28

1 SAMUEL

7:6	28
7:8	93
12:10	28
13:1–15	64
15:24	28
17	65
24—26	93

2 SAMUEL

6:20	25
7:6	96–97
12:13	28
19:21	28
24:10	28
24:16	97

1 KINGS

6:1	73
8	73
8:10–13	97
8:47	28
11—12	73
13:1–25	43
17:8–24	50, 86

2 KINGS

5:1–15	50
5:1–19	86

6:1–17	121
19:9	93
25:9	97

1 CHRONICLES

16:35	93

2 CHRONICLES

3:1	97
7:11–14	46

JOB

4:20	28
5:17–18	5, 46
5:22–23	126
7:12	125
8:1–22	43
9:8	83
9:13	125
11:6	43
22:1–30	43
24:19	27
25:6	28
26:13	125
40:15–24	125

PSALMS

8	20, 26
8:4	10
8:5	5
8:5–9	10
8:6	18
9:18	27
16:10	27
18:16	83
20:7	65
25:22	77
26:11	77
29:10	82
30:4	27
30:11	144
31:18	27
33:16–17	65
41:5	28
49:16	27
51:6	28
55:16	27
66	73

68	73	33:20–22	105	65:20	125
68:17	97	33:24	125	65:25	81, 126
74	73	35:1–7	48	66:3	102
74:12–17	82	35:3–4	94–95	**JEREMIAH**	
74:13	125	35:4	47	4:14	103
74:13–14	125	35:5–6	47–48,	7:4	97
76:3	97		76	8:21–22	39
77	73, 82	38:16	46–47	17:13–14	38–39
77:19	83	40	73, 104	31:31–34	103
78:38–39	28	40—55	95	31:34	56
78:69–70	97	40—66	73	32:20–21	47
80	73, 82	40:3	76, 132		
86:13	27	40:9	75, 95,	**EZEKIEL**	
88:6	27		104	8—10	97
89:10	125	40:12–31	75	34:16	46
103:2–6	45	41:1–10	75	37:1–14	140–41
103:13–14	28	41:14	77	47	98
104:26	125	42:1	104	**DANIEL**	
105	73	42:13	74	4:2–3	47
107:23–32	83	43:1	77	6	69
132:13	97	43:16	83	6:27	47
139:14	5	43:20–21	77	9:9	55
147:1–5	45– 46	43:25	55	11:2	141
PROVERBS		44:9–20	75	12:1	124
3:28–35	43	45:23	75	12:1–3	141
11:19	43	46:1–13	75	**HOSEA**	
13:13–23	43	49:6	74	1:9	68
		49:7	77	2:23	68
ISAIAH		51:9–10	83	6:1–3	140
1:6	40	51:9–11	125	11:1	75
2:1–5	40	52:7	104–5	**JOEL**	
4:3	141	52:7–8	95	2	124
5:14	27	53:4	76	2:28–32	139
11:1–5	55	53:5	46	**JONAH**	
11:1–9	40	53:6–12	76	1	83
11:6–9	55, 126	55:11	75	3:4	86
12:3	39	56—66	136	3:5–10	87
24:23	105	57:19	58	4:11	86
25:6	126	60	97	**MICAH**	
26:19	140	61:1	104	7:18	55
27:1	81–82,	61:1–2	48, 76,	**NAHUM**	
	125		104	1:4	82
30:26	46–47	64:5	39		
30:33	105	65	104		
32:1	105	65:17	90		
33:17	105				

HABAKKUK
3:15   83

ZEPHANIAH
3:17–20   39

ZECHARIAH
6:12–13   97

MALACHI
3:16–18   141

MATTHEW
1:21   76
1:23   76
2   75
2:15   75
3:1–3   76
3:11–12   106
4:1–10   76
4:1–11   83
5:20   57
6:12   28
6:15   56
8—9   44
8:1–4   44
8:5–13   76
8:17   76
9:2–8   44
9:9–13   44
9:27–31   44
11:2–3   106
11:2–5   48
11:2–6   83
11:5   76
12:22–30   83
12:24–33   48
20:28   76, 110–11
21:43   76
24:43   124
25:1–13   124
26:28   56
28:18–20   76
28:20   76

MARK
1:1   103
1:4–8   104

1:9–11   104
1:12–13   104
1:13   55, 83, 125–26
1:14   94
1:14–15   103–4
1:21–28   83
2:1–12   44
2:13–17   106–7
2:22–30   48
3:22–27   83
5:1–20   83
5:25–34   43
5:34   58
6:7–13   50
6:45–51   82
7:24–30   83
7:37   48
9:14–29   83
10:45   110–11
13   124
13:1   101
13:2   101
13:24   124
13:34–36   124
14:3–9   111

LUKE
1:46–55   63–64, 88
1:47   5
1:51   108
1:52   69
1:53   108
1:77   109
2:1–20   88
2:11   139
2:14   58
2:22–38   101
2:34–35   94
2:38   77
3:1–20   115
3:1–14   115
3:3   109
3:4   132

3:7–14   118
3:10   95
3:10–14   7, 108, 113–15
3:12   95, 108
3:14   95
3:16–17   106
4   50
4:1–13   83
4:16–30   86, 109
4:18–19   48, 108
5:1–11   130
5:14   43
5:20–21   109
5:23–24   109
5:27–32   107–9
5:32   108
6:12–49   130
6:24   108
6:35–36   117
6:36   56
7:18–20   106
7:18–22   48
7:18–23   83
7:21–22   121
7:29   108
7:47–49   109
7:50   58
8:10   130
8:26–39   43
8:41   108
8:49   108
9   130
9:23   116
9:44   130
9:45   130
9:51—19:48 130–31
10:25–37   87
11:1–13   117
11:4   28, 56, 109
11:14–23   83
11:14–26   48
11:15   83
11:17–22   83

11:20	48–49	8:28	110	4:9	137
11:29–32	94	9	44, 121	4:10	138
11:32	87	12:32–33	110	4:10–12	138
11:47–51	94	14:1–11	110	4:12	137
12:10	109	18:32	110	4:14	137
12:13–21	108	20:19–29	110	4:24–30	143
12:35–38	124	20:30–31	110	4:30	47, 138
12:42–48	124			4:31—5:11	138
13:1–4	121	**ACTS**		4:32–35	143
13:10–17	83–84,	1:8	142	5:12	47
	109	1:14	138	5:16	137
13:14	108	2:1	138	5:28	138
14	108	2:19	47	5:31	56, 115,
14:12–14	108	2:21	137		137–
14:13–14	122	2:22	47		39
14:15	126	2:25–31	139	5:40	138
14:15–24	121–22	2:32	139	5:41	138
15:1–2	108–9	2:33	139	6:8	47
16:19–31	108	2:33–36	50	7	116, 143
17:3–4	109	2:36	138	7:8	142
17:25	94	2:37	7, 95,	7:10	137
18:9–14	108		113	7:25	137
18:18–30	108	2:38	29, 94,	7:32	142
18:34	131		115,	7:34	137
19:1–10	108–9		117,	7:36	47
19:7	108		138–	7:51–53	94
19:9	108		39	8	142
19:10	108	2:40	93, 137	8:6	47
22:25	88	2:41	115	8:7	137
23:1–5	49	2:42–47	117,	8:12	115
23:34	56, 109		142–	8:13	47
24:47	109		43	8:16	138
		2:43	47	8:36	115
JOHN		2:44	115	9:1–19	117
1:1–14	100	2:44–45	138	9:2	132
1:29	100	2:47	137	9:14	138
3:1–15	110	3:1–10	50	9:16	138
3:1–21	109–10	3:6	138	9:17	139
3:10	110	3:12–16	50	9:18	115
3:14–15	110	3:12–26	142	9:21	138
3:15–16	136	3:13	142	9:34	50, 137
3:16	109	3:16	40, 115,	10:1—11:18	142
3:17	109		137	10:9	143
3:19–20	100	3:19	56, 115	10:33	143
3:36	136	3:20	126	10:38	137
5:24	136	4:2	140	10:43	138

10:43–44	139	17:3	114	6:14	29
10:47–48	115, 118	17:25	137	6:16–23	29
11:14	137–39	17:30	29, 115	6:19–23	59
11:15–17	139	17:30–31	142	6:23	29
11:15–18	138	18:8	115	7:14	29
11:17	115	19:8–10	114	8:4	132
11:18	115, 143	19:13	138	8:9	132
12:11	137	19:23	132	8:15–23	57
12:18–19	113	20:21	115	8:18–25	136
13:2	143	20:24	94	8:19–21	11, 125
13:16	114	21:13	138	8:23	131
13:16–41	116, 143	22:3	116	8:29	21
13:23	137	22:4	132	15:16	94
13:26	137–39	22:16	138	15:18–19	50
13:28	138	23:24	137	16:20	58
13:38	114	23:27	137		
13:39	115	26:17	137	**1 CORINTHIANS** 4	
13:41	114	26:17–18	114	1:7	136
13:43	56	26:20	115	1:10	134
13:47	137	27:20	137	1:18	94, 129
14:3	47	27:31	137	1:26–29	30
14:9	115, 137	27:34	137	3:12–13	132
14:14–15	50	27:43	137	3:18–19	30
14:15–16	114	27:44	137	4:9–13	30
15:1	137	28:1	137	5:7	77
15:7	115	28:4	137	5:9–11	30
15:7–9	138	28:8	137	10:1–4	77
15:7–11	115	28:9	137	11:7	20
15:8	139	28:27	137	11:17–34	143
15:11	137	28:28	137	11:29–30	43
15:12	47			12	50
16	142	**ROMANS**		15	136
16:14–15	118	1:1	94	15:1–11	134
16:15	115	1:18–32	29–30	15:12–34	134
16:16–18	50	3:23	28–29	15:24–28	136
16:23–40	113–14	3:24	77	15:35–58	134
16:23	113	5:1–2	58, 129–	15:38–58	134
16:24	113		30	15:49	21
16:27	113	5:1–10	53	16:22	136
16:28–34	118	5:1–11	112	**2 CORINTHIANS**	
16:30	7, 113, 137	5:8	112	1:22	132
		5:10	53	2:15	129
16:30–31	115	5:12—8:3	29	3:18	21
16:31	113–14, 137	5:12	29	4:4	21
		6:4	132–33	5:1–10	136
16:32	113	6:12	29	5:5	132

5:7	132
5:14—6:13	54, 112
5:16–17	86, 116
5:16–18	136
5:17	54, 125, 136
5:18–20	145
5:18–21	53
5:19	53, 94, 112
11:7	94
12:7	51
12:12	50

GALATIANS

3:10–14	87
3:28	85–86
4:3	85
4:5	57
4:9	85
4:13	51
5:22–23	132
6:9	132
6:15	54, 136
6:15–16	135

EPHESIANS

1:10	136
1:13	94
1:14	132
2:11–22	54, 135
2:15	136
2:17	87
4:13	133
4:23–24	136

PHILIPPIANS

1:6	132
1:27–30	88
2:6	21
2:6–11	75, 88
3:10–14	145
3:21	135–36
4:5	137

COLOSSIANS

1—2	85
1:5	94

1:13–14	85
1:15	21, 133
1:15–20	53–54, 136
1:21	87
1:24	125, 135
3:1–4	130
3:9–10	136
3:9–11	132
3:15	58

1 THESSALONIANS

1:5	50
1:9–10	131
2:2	94
2:8	94
2:9	94
2:11–13	131
3—4	59
4:1–17	131
5:2	124
5:4	124
5:23	131

1 TIMOTHY

1:11	94

PHILEMON 54

HEBREWS

2:10	60
4:15	59
5:7	60
5:7–9	60
7:26	59–60
7:28	60
9:25–28	100
9:28	136
10:10	100
10:12–14	100
11:1	129

JAMES

1:13–14	29
1:21	51
1:27	29
2:5	29
2:13	51

2:14–26	57
2:23	29
3:6	29
3:9	20–21
3:13	51
3:17	51
4:1–4	29
4:4	29
4:11–12	51
5:8	136–37
5:13–16	51
5:14–16	51
5:15	51
5:16	51
5:19	51
5:20	51

1 PETER

1:3–5	129
1:3–12	76
1:15–16	58
2:2	132
2:9–10	77
2:10	68
2:17	88
4:17	94

2 PETER

3:1–18	127
3:10	124
3:13	125
3:13–14	127

REVELATION

1:4	127
1:8	127
1:17	127
2:3	92
2:7	91
2:10	92
2:11	91
2:13	127
2:17	91
2:25	92
2:26	91
3:5	92
3:12	92

3:21	127
4—5	127–28
4:8	127
4:9	137
4:10	137
4:11	90
5	91, 129
5:9–10	92
6:16	127
7:9	127
7:9–10	135
7:9–11	87
7:14	124
10:6	137
11:17	127
11:18	91
12:7–10	81
12:9	91
12:11	92
13:1–10	91
13:10	92
13:11–18	91
14:12	92
15—16	91
15:1–5	91
15:2	91
15:5	91
15:7	137
16:5	127
16:15	124
17:14	91
18:4	91
18:12–13	89
19:9	126
19:10	92
20:2	91
21—22	137
21:1	11, 55, 82, 90
21:4	125, 144
21:5	90
21:6	127
21:7	91
22:5	136
22:13	127
22:20	136

Printed in the United States
135879LV00003B/150/A